# LITERACY

# OUT

# LOUD

*Creating vibrant classrooms where "talk"
is the springboard for all learning*

TERRY ANNE CAMPBELL

MICHELLE E. MCMARTIN

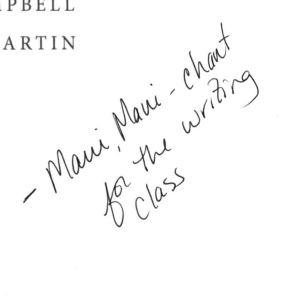

*– Maui, Maui – chant
for the writing
class*

Pembroke Publishers Limited

*To the fabulous kids in Michelle's Grade 3–4 class who provided us
with countless LOL moments!*

**© 2017 Pembroke Publishers**
538 Hood Road
Markham, Ontario, Canada L3R 3K9
www.pembrokepublishers.com

Distributed in the U.S. by Stenhouse Publishers
PO Box 11020
Portland, ME 04104-7020
www.stenhouse.com

**Library and Archives Canada Cataloguing in Publication**

Campbell, Terry Anne, author
    Literacy out loud : creating vibrant classrooms where "talk" is the springboard
for all learning / Terry Anne Campbell & Michelle E. McMartin.

Issued in print and electronic formats.
ISBN 978-1-55138-323-1 (softcover).--ISBN 978-1-55138-924-0 (PDF)

    1. Children--Language. 2. Oral communication. 3. Reading (Elementary).
4. Language arts (Elementary). I. McMartin, Michelle E. author II. Title.

LB1139.L3C34 2017          372.62'2 C2017-903688-2
C2017-903689-0

Editor: Kate Revington
Cover Design: John Zehethofer
Typesetting: Jay Tee Graphics Ltd.

Printed and bound in Canada
9 8 7 6 5 4 3 2 1

# Contents

**Introduction: Why Classroom Talk Matters**  *5*

Oral Language: A Constant Becoming Yet More Important  *6*
The *It* Factor of Literacy  *6*
Positive Emotional Connections Through Talk  *7*
Oral Language: "Like a Compass"  *8*

**Chapter 1: Using Oral Language to Create Community**  *9*

The Impetus of Thought  *9*
Community Circle: Setting the Tone for the Day  *11*
Passing the Talking Stick  *15*
Building Community Through Story Sharing  *16*
Thoughts on Creating a Community That Is Caring  *17*

**Chapter 2: Creating a "Talk" Classroom**  *19*

Why Teachers May Mistrust Talk  *19*
Having Real Discussions with Our Students  *21*
On the Need for a "Good Talk" Model  *23*
Strategies for Cultivating Good Talk  *23*
Assessing Talk: Part of Purposeful Planning  *27*
Conditions for Creating a Classroom Where Talk Flourishes  *29*
The Last Word: Students Talk About Talk  *30*

**Chapter 3: Learning Out Loud: Talk Strategies for Students**  *31*

Sketch to Stretch *Plus*  *31*
The Strategy Applied to *The Crow's Tale*  *33*
Working with Wordless Books  *38*
Discussion Strategies for Partners  *40*
Small-Group Discussion Strategies  *41*
Whole-Group Discussions and Sharing  *44*
Close Connections: Talking and Drawing  *45*

**Chapter 4: Playing with Language Out Loud**  *47*

Let's Begin with Poetry  *48*
Creating Multimodal Poetry  *48*
Using Texts to Spark Thought and Talk about Words  *53*
Playing with Words to Augment Vocabulary  *55*

**Chapter 5: Optimizing the Impact of Read-Alouds**   *59*

Take Students on a Reading Ride   *59*
Provocative Texts and Talking About Them   *62*
Problem-Based Texts   *66*
Evocative Texts: Where Visuals Stimulate Conversation   *68*
Strategies for Use Before, During, and After the Read-Aloud   *71*
The Last Word: Students Talk About Read-Alouds   *72*

**Chapter 6: Using Drama to Enhance Oral Communication**   *75*

Not Quiet on the Set! Drama Produces Better Communication   *76*
Choral Speaking — No Two Oral Interpretations Alike   *77*
Everyday Drama Activities   *80*
Using Minimal Scripts for Maximum Effect   *81*
Exploring the Potential of Nursery Rhymes   *82*
Asking Questions, Composing Answers   *83*
What to Strive For in the Drama Classroom   *85*

**Chapter 7: Speaking from the Heart: Storytelling**   *89*

Cultural Considerations in Story Selection   *89*
Benefits of Engaging in Storytelling   *91*
Getting Started in Storytelling   *92*
Storytelling in a Range of Ways   *93*
Fire from the Spoken Word   *101*

**Chapter 8: Using Talk Circles for Readers Theatre**   *103*

What Readers Theatre Does   *104*
Getting Started with Readers Theatre   *105*
Demonstration of Readers Theatre with Critical Listeners   *106*
Ten Steps for Successful Readers Theatre   *108*
Co-creating Scripts   *110*

**Chapter 9: Coming Full Circle**   *115*

The Beauty of the Circle   *115*
Talking Like Walking: Students' Voices   *117*

Acknowledgments   *119*
References   *121*
Index   *125*

# Introduction: Why Classroom Talk Matters

*Why does talk matter? Classroom talk shapes and is shaped by the classroom learning environment. Through talk patterns, teachers demonstrate and discover what they expect and value, just as students discover and demonstrate what counts in terms of learning, knowledge, and knowing.*

— *Maureen Boyd and Lee Galda, 2011, pp. 2–3*

Since 2008, we, the authors, have been working together to investigate effective literacy practices. We have been talking together, teaching and learning together, and marvelling at the creativity and learning potential we experience when engaging with the students in Michelle's classrooms. We have explored and written about storytelling and story writing, too (Campbell & Hlusek, 2009, 2015). And the more we have inquired into classroom literacy practices, the more rooted our belief in the central role of *oral language communication* has become.

We both feel that the time is right for describing a "talk," or dialogic, classroom, where oral language strategies take centre stage. With the increasing demands, challenges, and distractions of the digital realities facing learners today, the ability to both navigate the technological world and achieve a balance with other dimensions of our lives has become essential. As part of this balance, we see effective face-to-face speaking and listening skills as necessary for healthy social relationships and mental well-being. To flourish as learners and as human beings, we need to be articulate oral communicators. Teachers can cultivate this ability in students through vibrant classroom talk.

We would argue that oral language matters in our classrooms, perhaps more than ever. Here are three key reasons:

1. Full participation in 21st-century literacies requires oral language communication and, indeed, puts special focus on oral modes of communication.
2. Oral language is an essential part of literacy learning. Reading, writing, talk, and related multiliteracies flourish together under the same conditions.
3. Effective listening and speaking in social contexts is the foundation of *all* learning, especially in a "talk" classroom such as we advocate, contributing to a healthy, vibrant classroom community.

## Oral Language: A Constant Becoming Yet More Important

The literacy landscape has been changing in our lives and in our classrooms. The meaning of the term *literacy* now embraces more than the traditional pillars of reading, writing, and oral communication; it encompasses digital technologies where *multimodal texts*, or texts where written modes are combined "with oral, visual, audio, gestural, tactile and spatial patterns of meaning" (Kalantzis & Cope, 2012, p. 2), are prevalent. Here, and throughout this text, literacy is recognized in its traditional sense and in the current sense of *multiple* literacies, which encompasses our contemporary communication environment.

Despite game-changing developments, *oral language* remains a constant. Learning a spoken language is the beginning of literacy, and listening and speaking remain fundamental to learning of all kinds. Oral language lies at the heart of becoming and being literate. In fact, some argue that in this era of new literacies, oral language is more important than ever:

> New overlays of oral and written modes emerge as email and text messaging more closely resemble the fluidity of speaking than the earlier literate forms of letters and memoranda. (Kalantzis & Cope, 2012, p. 35)

As the quotation indicates, the "fluidity of speaking" spills over into present-day communication methods, from texting to social media messages. Our students need to be fluent oral language users to use new platforms effectively, so that they can navigate the 21st-century literacy landscape.

With its focus on oral language use, *Literacy Out Loud* bears in mind the necessity of developing reading and writing abilities along with 21st-century literacies. The book offers strategies that focus on oral language and helps to foster related skills through engaging activities. It describes literacy activities and events that take place through listening and speaking — they occur *out loud*. The title has the acronym *LOL*, which, in social media parlance, means "laugh out loud." Accordingly, the goal of having fun — enjoyable, social learning — is deliberately emphasized. Listening and speaking — or *talk*, for short — is the lifeblood of a vibrant classroom. It makes learning possible. It is the *it* factor of literacy.

## The *It* Factor of Literacy

It makes sense to continue to promote the language arts of listening and speaking in our classrooms. Language is learned in use, in a wide range of social and emotional relationships and contexts. One naturally occurring context is *conversation*. Marie Clay urges teachers to "understand that children learn language easily through conversation." She goes on to remind us that "a young learner's control over language must expand." For this to happen, we must "[c]reate the need to produce language. Tempt children to have something to say. This happens naturally in shared activities that call for the exchange of language" (Clay, 2004, p. 10).

Literacy flourishes as oral language develops; oral language is the continuous vehicle and accompaniment for all literacy learning. Listening and speaking are essential for building a community of learners and for supporting literacy learners in all their diversity.

"Oral language is the foundation of literacy development: there is a common base serving all three activities of talking, reading, and writing."
— Marie Clay, 2004, p. 4

## What Brain Imaging Reveals

Oral communication cannot be taught as a separate strand of literacy. It is not a side dish; rather, it is an integral part of literacy learning. Consider that when people learn and use oral language, the same parts of the brain are involved as when they engage in other literacy activities. "The oral and written forms of language are only superficially different . . .," writes Brian Cambourne, the influential Australian educator. "The same neural processes are involved, using the same neural machinery" (1988, pp. 28–29). This assertion is backed up by brain imaging that shows "reading relies on brain circuits already in place for language" (Shaywitz, 2003, p. 67).

Buchweitz (2016) reports that "a brain imaging study of four different languages (Spanish, English, Hebrew, and Chinese) showed the universality of the language network in the brain. In all languages, the traditional left frontal-temporal network of the brain was activated for listening comprehension . . ." The study also showed "a common brain signature for reading in the four languages." Furthermore, "once children learn to read, the centers for processing print are grafted onto a left-lateralized network of language areas hardwired for spoken language" (2016, p. S10).

When we combine these facts with the way language is learned in use, in social settings, then we can see that promoting listening and speaking activities as part of our everyday literacy practices in the classroom makes more sense than treating reading, writing, and oral communication as separate curricular categories.

How can teachers best create a lively social network of literacy learning where *talk* is the foundation? How can classroom talk be encouraged and guided so that students become fluent and effective oral communicators? This book proposes everyday activities intended to answer these questions.

## Positive Emotional Connections Through Talk

*Why start your day with talk?* Dr. Judy Willis, a neurologist and a classroom teacher, makes a strong argument for doing this. She writes about the emotional and social connections in learning and memory. She explains, "When a student cares about new information or learning, it forms new synaptic connections and is stored as a long-term memory . . . Positive neural circuit connecting occurs when the lesson is associated with a positive emotional experience." And then she concludes, "This positive emotional experience can be the result of feelings of accomplishment, *pleasant social interactions with classmates or the teacher, or specific acknowledgment and praise*" (2006, p. 21, emphasis added).

These insights can be applied to the recommended practice of beginning each day with Community Circle. As elaborated upon in Chapter 1, Community Circle, with its circle formation, gives all learners equal status and allows students to readily see and hear one another. Michelle has made it the foundation of her oral language and community-building practice. She further promotes positive discussions by the use of a smooth stone, which is passed from speaker to speaker. This ritual encourages the practice of taking turns and the focus on one main conversation to which students have an opportunity to contribute.

### The Effect of Discussion Equity

Brain research shows that if you have a positive conversation, there is an increase in the release of dopamine. *Discussion equity*, by making positive conversations possible during Community Circle, engages dopamine in the brain. Dopamine plays a role in motivation and reinforcement. Lively, relevant, and engaging

As authors, we are a collaborative team. In this resource, we draw on experiences in Michelle's classrooms — she has taught Grades 3 to 8 in Northern Ontario — and experiences of teacher candidates working with Terry as a teacher educator at Nipissing University. Terry has served as a classroom teacher, as well, and is a welcome visitor in Michelle's classrooms.

conversation enables students to start the day with a positive feeling and to be motivated to learn throughout the day.

Talk in this setting is valuable for its own sake, as a community builder, and as a condition of well-being, which requires positive communication experiences (Shankar, 2013). But talk is beneficial in other (connected) ways, as well. One benefit involves the deeper connections to literacy development.

## Oral Language: "Like a Compass"

As teachers, we know that our students learn by doing. The more they read — for pleasure and for purpose — the better they become as readers. The more they write, the better they become at expressing their thoughts and feelings in written forms that can be shared, including multimodal or digital creations. They then realize how the texts they create can have an impact. Fluent oral language skills contribute to progress in reading and writing. But how can we make this happen for all the learners in our classrooms? Engaging in stimulating oral language activities can entice learners to read more often by choice. Classroom talk can inspire more writing of higher quality; it also plays a key role in various forms of text production because most often, learning how to use technology occurs alongside peers. Classroom talk enhances literacy skills of all kinds. Furthermore, being orally articulate is part of being literate.

Although literacy begins long before children enter formal schooling, once they come through our doorways, we are responsible for cultivating oral language and ensuring that literacy flourishes. As a teacher candidate completing her final placement in an Early Learning Kindergarten (ELK) class, Whitney Underhill commented:

"When observing very young learners in ELK, I noticed that oral language is like a compass. Young children use it to navigate new situations and tasks, as well as to direct themselves back through memories — through places they have already been. Just like a compass, using oral language takes practice, and I notice young children repeating new words that they have heard, sometimes singing the word, in order to ingrain it into their memory. This is not unlike studying a new route, mapping compass points in order to be able to use that route again to get to a desired location. Very young children use oral language to navigate a world that is still brand new to them."

Classroom talk strategies, at the core of this text, create the following opportunities for all students:

- to engage in speaking and listening for fun and for finding out things about themselves, one another, and their world
- to become alert to the many topics they can talk about, read about, and write about collaboratively and individually
- to find their own voice through listening attentively and responding genuinely

In sum, engaging in dynamic classroom talk is essential in its own right and makes all learning possible. That is the focus of this text.

# 1

## Using Oral Language to Create Community

*A finch woke up in the dark and the quiet. He had a thought, and he heard it. I AM HENRY FINCH, he thought. I THINK, he thought.*

— *Alexis Deacon*, I Am Henry Finch

*When I first came into this class two months ago, the morning Community Circle helped me fit in. There's some time before announcements just before the real circle begins, when we can just sit and chat about what we did on the weekend or whatever. That's how I made new friends.*

— *Larry, Grade 3 student*

When human beings speak, they are saying, *I am*.

Through speaking, we express the fact that we are thinking and feeling, and that we can communicate this to other thinking, feeling beings. When we listen to one another, we become aware of the thoughts and feelings of other human beings. This is at the core of community life.

### The Impetus of Thought

*I Am Henry Finch* by Alexis Deacon is a picture book about a finch named Henry, who lives in a raucous flock of finches, all portrayed by illustrator Viviane Schwarz as bright red fingerprints. The birds are constantly chattering, but don't seem to have much deep to say. One night, though, something happens: Henry has a thought! Henry begins to be aware of his own thoughts and considers his existence as a thinking, feeling individual. It is an existential moment. One powerful result of it includes Henry's newfound ability to communicate with — and thereby cleverly tame — the beast that threatened the flock. After his Jonah-like adventure in the belly of the beast, "Henry told the finches about everything that had happened, and they listened." This event results in a second powerful outcome: the finches begin to have thoughts and to express those thoughts; they thereby discover that they have individual identities. They fly off to have adventures of their own. "We will come back!" they call out as they leave. *Great*, thought Henry.

Touchstone texts are "all types of texts that are read, viewed, or experienced on multiple occasions over time. These texts become part of the collective narrative of a classroom community" (Parr & Campbell, 2012, p. 5).

When introduced to *I Am Henry Finch*, Terry's teacher candidates quickly agreed that it would make a great *touchstone text* in any elementary classroom (K–8). The use of fingerprint art is an obvious response activity. One teacher candidate tried out the text in Michelle's Grade 3–4 class. She read the text aloud and held a *grand conversation*, or a large-group discussion of the key themes of the text. She then engaged the students in fingerprint art. Since the teacher candidates had been told not to ask their students to do anything they were not willing to do, too, the student teacher produced this post-listening response. Artwork by a Grade 3 student follows.

*This response by the student teacher in Michelle's classroom shows a group of finches, each beginning to think independent thoughts. Notice that it provides commentary on the book, written as though the finches are voicing their opinions.*

*With its vivid red finches and thought bubbles, this painting shows a Grade 3 student's detailed response to* I Am Henry Finch. *Notice how the birds and other animals think in their own voices, for example, the one blue bird saying, "What am I?" and the blue reindeer asking, "Is it Christmas?" In some places, invented spelling is used.*

The fact that the story of Henry Finch can be a metaphor for a joyful, chattering classroom of individual students is obvious. But how can we raise classroom chatter to higher levels of thinking and communicating while maintaining the joy of talking together? How can joyful conversations contribute to both individual identity and to the creation of a thriving classroom community? Our hope is that we can maintain the fun inherent in socializing together while learning as we provide opportunities for learners to raise their thinking levels and develop more sophisticated language use individually and as a community.

## The Challenges of Managing Talk

Many teachers have second thoughts about encouraging talk in their classrooms. Some still see a quiet, orderly classroom as the ideal of good teacher management. At the same time, most recognize the importance of healthy conversation and discussion as part of learning in a social setting. How can we balance our accountability as teachers with a willingness to relinquish control and let our students talk? How can we manage talk so that it doesn't grow too loud, get too out of hand, or drift off-topic? How can we channel the energy of the loud talkers so that they do not dominate every discussion? At the other extreme, how can we ensure that the quiet members of our community have a voice and are listened to? Furthermore, how can we help to shape classroom talk in ways that foster deeper thinking and promote better communication skills? These are perennial teaching questions, whether we teach young children or adults.

*Literacy Out Loud* addresses these questions with specific strategies, most notably Community Circle, which both authors have used successfully.

*or a Restorative Circle*

## Community Circle: Setting the Tone for the Day

Sitting in a circle affords all participants equal status. As listeners, students can all see one another. As speakers, students do not need to speak too loudly. Speakers will take turns around the sharing circle.

In Community Circle, a talking stick — or, as in Michelle's classroom, a smooth stone that fits easily into the hand — can be passed from speaker to speaker, indicating that only the person holding the talking stick has the privilege of speaking. Using this approach encourages taking turns. For the first round, at least, it seems to prevent any one person from dominating the conversation or side conversations from developing. That may be because it is so obvious who is speaking when.

In Michelle's classroom, every single day begins with Community Circle. The rest of the day may bring interruptions and changes to routines, but the daily ritual of circle time is far too important to overlook.

For ease of reference, we will refer to the object that a designated speaker holds as a *talking stick*. Indeed, Terry uses a hand-carved talking stick. The use of a talking stick has long been associated with both community building and storytelling. However, any object can be passed from speaker to speaker.

## Within and Around the Circle: Michelle's Model

Michelle has a talking stone ready to be passed on from speaker to speaker. She also has a box of quotations, questions, and identified social dilemmas, one of which will be chosen to be the focus of that day's circle. Here are three examples:

- Frederick, in the book by Leo Lionni, claims that what he does — gathering sunrays — is work. Do you agree? Why do you think that?

Circles represent interconnectedness, equality, and continuity — important principles in Indigenous worldview and belief systems. According to traditional teaching, the seasonal pattern of life and renewal, as well as the movement of animals and people, is continuous, like a circle, which has no beginning and no end. Circles are found throughout nature. They suggest inclusiveness and lack of a hierarchy.

Another kind of circle is the Socratic circle. As the Colorin Colorado project for English language learners puts it:

"A Socratic circle, also known as Socratic seminar, is a teaching strategy used to support deep understanding of a specific piece of writing, music, or art. It is based on Socrates' belief in the importance of developing students' ability to think critically and independently through the use of dialogue."

*Socratic Circles: Fostering Critical and Creative Thinking in Middle and High School*, by Matt Copeland, offers help on using this kind of circle in the classroom.

- If you were a circus performer, what would you be and why?
- If you had a friend over to your house and that friend always left your room a mess, how would you feel, and what would you say or do about the problem?

The stone is passed round-robin style around the circle, with students encouraged to talk but given the option to pass.

Michelle involves the students in setting up the circle over time. At first, in September, she sets up the chairs, including a special one for the day's leader, around a blanket and also places any props, such as a feather and candle; however, she encourages the students to take over. By January, setup happens on its own each morning because of the atmosphere that has been created. The students respect one another because of their daily personal contact which includes shaking hands. Because of the circle formation, no one can be excluded. Michelle teaches them to make eye contact and to shake hands firmly and respectfully. It sets the tone for the day.

## Moral Teachings

The central value is respect. At the beginning of the year, Michelle asks the class what this is, and the students make up rules based on their understanding, which evolves throughout the year. Just as virtually every religion teaches respect for one another, the practice of holding Community Circle, where everyone talks together and greets one another, promotes respect.

Do what is suitable for your community — the only rule is respect. Students accept that all practices, rules, and behaviors are fundamentally about this.

Since Ojibwe tradition is relevant to Michelle's classroom, laminated footprint images, each with one of the Seven Sacred Grandfather teachings, are placed in the centre. The seven principles are Honesty, Bravery, Respect, Truth, Wisdom, Humility, and Love. The values are to govern student and teacher interactions. They are introduced and discussed in context through read-alouds that exemplify certain teachings as well as through Community Circle questions. Sometimes, the teacher may think a book is about Wisdom, for instance, but students may think it is about Respect — that becomes a rich discussion focus. "It's an organic process over time," says Michelle.

## Symbolic Objects at the Centre

Choice of symbolic objects, or props, varies depending on what is being discussed that day or emphasized that week. A good kind of object to place on the blanket or rug and refer to is anything that will help unify the students, for example, a quilt made by the class.

One item used in Michelle's classroom is a candle. It is lit daily while students share and think about people who need positive thoughts, even prayers, because they may, for example, be ill.

Another item often featured is a feather, which is metaphorical for any moral teaching. In Michelle's classroom, it has Indigenous significance. The spine of the feather represents the central path towards the Grandfather teachings while the feather strands suggest how people stray and make choices away from the centre. The fact that spine and strands are all joined as one indicates that people can always return to the central path. The feather can be readily used in character traits or character education.

*Going Around the Circle*

Once the children are in their seats, Michelle enters the circle as one of the participants. Some days, she goes around the circle and simply asks how each child is feeling that morning. One word responses are okay. No comments are needed. In this way, everyone knows that J. has not had a good start to his day and is feeling down or that M. has something to celebrate and feels joyful.

The leader of the day chooses just one prepared card to be discussed that day and reads the question or quotation (with help from a peer or Michelle, if needed).

Beginning with the leader, the stone is passed, and each participant shares feelings and thoughts about the question or quotation chosen. Circle members are allowed to pass when they have nothing to say. No time limit applies.

"We take as long as we need to talk together that morning," reports Michelle.

Michelle uses the time to reinforce good discussion, compassion, kindness, and support for one another's thoughts, feelings, and efforts. The students often congratulate one another on something attempted or achieved.

There is always laughter.

The class finishes the circle by standing, doing a walkaround of handshaking, and saying "*Migwetch*" (which is "thank you" in Ojibwe). They then pick up their chairs and move them to the table group of their choice.

**Thank You!**

Of course, another form of daily greeting can be used. Every child may shake hands and make eye contact with every other child and say something like "Have a good day" or "Thanks for listening to me today." Or, students could say one positive thing about each of their peers, even "You look great today!" The goal is to start the day with positive contact and acknowledgment.

---

### Ideas on Developing Questions for Community Circle

- Quotations chosen from daily read-alouds or from the students' independent reading can be recorded on cards to be chosen for discussion.
- Consider referring to *The Teacher's Toolkit* (Ontario Ministry of Education, 2009) to discover many discussion topics.
  (See www.edu.gov.on.ca)
- Check out *Tools for Life: Relationship Building Solutions*. This resource provides a "frame of reference for dealing with the ups and downs of relationships in school and beyond. Classroom management is less the issue. Better learning is the outcome." Sample questions and dilemmas for discussion are provided.
  (See http://toolsforliferesources.com/teachers/)
- For discussion topics relating to social problem solving, you may want to consider commercial sources such as *Social Thinking: Should I or Shouldn't I? What Would Others Think?* (Check out the Social Thinking website.)

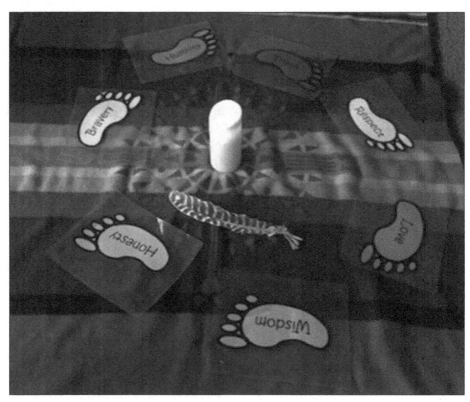

*The laminated footprints on the Community Circle rug remind students of the principles that are to govern their talk with one another.*

## The Value of Community Circle

"Our Community Circle is about developing a cultural community," explains Michelle. "It's about encouraging compassion and empathy, because it's a safe place to share feelings and ideas, where the students can be themselves.

"We simply could not begin our day without Community Circle. The day would be destroyed! I can't even imagine my class if we didn't have Community Circle first thing in the morning. It's like a family meeting. We are like one big family. We appreciate and respect each other. It's a chance to look one another in the eye and tell one another how we feel and what we think. If we don't hold the circle, the students are 'off' all day, and so am I."

Michelle's students value the use of Community Circle. Here are some of their comments:

- "I like Community Circle because everyone gets a chance to really talk: not just chatting, or random things, but to talk about how we are feeling, how to solve a problem, and things like that." (Ali)
- "I like when we pick a question, like what's your favorite movie, and we find other people who feel the same." (Mya)
- "We get to listen to each other and talk with some kids we might not talk to very much." (Mikko)
- "When I first came into this class two months ago, the morning Community Circle helped me fit in. There's some time before announcements just before the real circle begins, when we can just sit and chat about what we did on the weekend or whatever. That's how I made new friends." (Larry)

## Passing the Talking Stick

On one memorable day, Terry was an invited guest to Michelle's classroom. She brought her talking stick to show to the students. She explained the significance of her stick, a gift from the Storytellers of Canada, a national organization that supports the art of oral storytelling. The children understood that the stick was equivalent in purpose to the stone they normally used. Terry passed her stick around and invited each child to comment on the importance of talking. Here are some of the students' comments beginning with what a boy named Chris said when he held the stick:

> Well, you talk to communicate your feelings. You talk to solve problems, to share when good things happen and sometimes when bad things happen. You have to talk to do things like apologize when you do something wrong. But also, people will know what you are thinking. You can help make them understand you. There are situations where the only way to make people understand you is to talk. Mostly, you talk to communicate.

Many children picked up on talking to communicate. They mentioned sharing their feelings and emotions with one another, talking to understand one another. As Torry put it when he held the stick:

> We talk to understand. We talk for teaching. We talk and listen to learn.

Stick in hand, Ali, a loquacious and fluent speaker, said:

> I don't think talking is that important, because you can communicate other ways, too. Like sign language, texting, and writing. They are important ways to communicate, too.

Another student, Sadi, picked up on Ali's ideas. Holding the stick, she said:

> But you can express yourself more easily by talking and you can show how you feel at the same time, with your face, and your hands. When you write, you can't do that. I can think and feel more things than I can write. But I can say them more easily when I talk.

And as Julia grasped the stick, she mused:

*A student holds the talking stick, ready to speak.*

If we couldn't talk, we wouldn't be able to know what other people are feeling, or about what they know, what they are thinking . . .

## Building Community Through Story Sharing

In addition to the ritual of Community Circle, there are other ways in which oral language communication is the foundation of community building. Consider the following examples of linking oral language use with the development of a classroom community.

### Telling Stories from Oral Family Heritage

Before class, a mother from an Ojibwe family brought her eight-year-old son, Torry (pseudonym), to his new school in September and asked to meet his teacher, who was Michelle. The boy stood tall and straight and wore a beautiful long braid down his back. His mother offered to visit the class in the first week of school to tell her son's new classmates the story of the braided hair — how and why it is significant in their culture.

Later, Michelle described how the class was riveted, and how immediately, the boy was not only accepted, but was recognized for who he was. Throughout the school year, Torry often shared stories from his Ojibwe heritage, and his mother became a frequent visitor as a storyteller. Through storytelling, Torry became a central member of the classroom and school community.

### Finding Models in Read-Aloud Fictional Texts

A good idea is to read aloud a text such as *Marianthe's Story: Painted Words, Spoken Memories*. Doing so will give listeners much to respond to and tales to tell and talk about. One rich open-ended question to pose to Community Circle is "Think back to a situation where you were 'the new kid' and didn't know the language or the game being played. How did you feel?" *Marianthe's Story* is based on author Aliki Brandenburg's experiences as a young immigrant from Greece. The fictional character, Marianthe — Mari for short — arrives at her new school without a word of English. In the first half of the story, called *Painted Words*, Mari's teacher welcomes her with a handshake and a smile, and shows her the creating centre, where day after day Mari paints the story of herself and her family. One student comments, "Look! Mari is painting what she cannot say!"

Following her mother's instructions, Mari looks, listens, and learns. Over time, the sounds she hears the teacher and students make become words, and the words take on meanings. In the part of the story called *Spoken Memories*, Mari has learned how to tell her story in words. Using her paintings and her new language, she becomes a class storyteller, relating the story of her homeland, her family, and their journey to their new country. Her storytelling is greeted with loud bravos. But the victory is not only Marianthe's: she brings her new knowledge of written and spoken English home to her mother.

Terry has read this text many times to her B.Ed. students, a far more diverse group than the North Bay population generally, to great effect. There are many immigrants and children of immigrants from Europe, Africa, and Asia among her students. Many of them come from the Toronto area and do their teaching placements there, as well. These teacher candidates respond on deeply personal levels to Marianthe's story. There are often tears, especially when Mari shares her new knowledge of English with her mother. Several students have commented that this happened in their homes with parents or grandparents learning along with their children. Here is a representative writing sample from a teacher candidate, named Sophea, who identified this book as one of her touchstone texts (a course assignment):

*Title:* Marianthe's Story: Painted Words/Spoken Memories

*Author/Illustrator:* Aliki

*Synopsis:* Marianthe is a new student in a new school from a faraway country, and does not speak English. The story is about how she overcomes the language and cultural differences with the help of her teacher, her family, and her own creativity.

*Grade Level:* 3 or 4

*Teaching Potential:* This story is a great way to welcome new students, learning acceptance and ways of communicating. It teaches inclusiveness and the acceptance of others.

I chose this as a personal touchstone text because I came to Canada when I was four with my parents and grandparents. We are Cambodian, and I was born in a refugee camp in Thailand after my parents escaped from Cambodia. When I went to school in Toronto, I knew no English and felt very scared. But my Kindergarten teacher, like Mari's teacher, treated me kindly, and invited my mom and grandmother into the school. They learned English along with me. I found this story to be very moving and believable and cannot wait to share it when I am on placement in Toronto schools, where there are many immigrants with stories similar to mine and Mari's.

## Connecting to Families and Their Communities

Like the fictional character Marianthe and the First Nations boy Torry, children arrive in our classrooms with stories. Their stories tell who they are and where they come from. Their stories are an intrinsic part of them, as they enter and leave our classrooms, as they live and learn.

Tapping into these dynamic tales brings benefits. We can tap into them through invitations to family members to visit, student interviews, letters to families, and surveys of student interests early in the school year. Doing so will allow us to build relationships with our students as individuals and a sense of community among all members of the class. We can create a fund of stories worth reading, writing — and talking about. Today, these stories can be shared directly through such means as classroom blogs. In this way, the classroom community spills out into the entire school and beyond, to families and caregivers.

## Thoughts on Creating a Community That Is Caring

We have focused this chapter on using oral language to create community, but what kind of community will it be? Regie Routman (2003, p. 12) famously said, "Unless we reach into our students' hearts, we have no entry into their minds." In

In *Creating Caring Classrooms*, Kathleen Gould Lundy and Larry Swartz (2011, p. 10) say:

Our advice is to build community not only at the beginning of the year but all through it, and not as a separate event but woven into curriculum events. Looking after the learning community becomes part of the everyday work in the classroom, and as time goes by, barriers between students come down, and wonderful friendships and relationships are built.

To explore how to create community further, be sure to check out their first-rate resource.

this spirit and to help bring our discussion to an appropriate close, here are some of our thoughts about creating a caring, respectful classroom community.

- Begin communicating with families on day one, or before, if possible. Always show the utmost respect.
- Show your students that you care about them by listening to them carefully and by treating them with kindness and compassion.
- Discover students' interests and cultural backgrounds, perhaps inviting family members into the classroom. Incorporate what you learn from them into your classroom practice as much as possible.
- Be flexible with teaching and learning plans. When things don't go as expected, don't blame the students. The teacher's job is to think of a better plan or approach.
- Think of learning as a continuous cycle. As Michelle notes, "It's about practice as a whole, as a continuum, where one thing builds on another; it's about thinking well beyond individual lessons or units." We are teaching human individuals who are at different points in their learning and growth.
- Convey to your students that you believe they will succeed. If you do so, chances are they will.
- Provide rich tasks and expect them to rise to the occasion.
- Celebrate all successes and efforts with the whole class daily. Say, for example, "I like when you said . . .," or "I like when you did . . ." During sharing time, for instance, you might say something like "This is going to be really good because Chris knows about doing Stop Motion. He's so good!"
- Create an atmosphere where everyone feels free to express their thoughts and feelings without fear of feeling wrong. Pose many open-ended questions and topics, and encourage open-minded responses.
- Keep all students safe and healthy physically, socially, emotionally, spiritually, and cognitively.
- Approach all assessment processes with the highest ethical principles. Communicating assessment with students should always contribute to progress and well-being; it should never cause psychological harm or discouragement. "My mother is a doctor," Michelle observes, "and in the back of my mind is always the moral imperative, *do no harm*."

Talk in this setting is valuable for its own sake and as a community builder. But talk is beneficial in other ways as well. In Chapter 2, we explore the use of teacher talk in *real discussions* with our students. Through real discussions, we can get to know our students better — in all their diversity. We can then purposefully plan next steps for their learning experiences, including plans for supporting their growth as articulate communicators.

# 2

## Creating a "Talk" Classroom

*Talk is like the sea . . . talk surrounds us and constitutes our primary mode of action. It is our medium, our atmosphere, and also our substance.*

*— D. L. Rubin, 1990, p. 3*

*Talk is like music. Your mouth is an instrument.*
*You're expressing the song of your emotions.*

*— Lucy and Ali, Grade 3 students*

In Chapter 1, we presented classroom talk as a condition of community building and focused on the strategy of using community sharing circles. As the Rubin quotation says, "Talk is like the sea." Rubin is alluding to a quotation by James Britton (1970): "Talk is the sea upon which all else floats." He goes on to say, "Like the sea, talk is the environment that first incubates and then nurtures our development." If talk is the medium for all learning, then how can we as teachers ensure that talk is used in the classroom to its full potential? Where do we go beyond beginning each day with Community Circle? How can we create a "talk," or dialogic, classroom, where there is ongoing, genuinely conversational talk between teacher and students?

### Why Teachers May Mistrust Talk

Let's begin by examining some of the reasons teachers may hesitate to employ talk as fully as they might, even though it is recognized as a fundamental learning vehicle. First, teachers may find it uncomfortable to relinquish control and allow the students to talk, particularly when their talk sounds superficial and off-topic. Yet it is our responsibility to plan purposefully and to ensure that students are learning and meeting academic expectations as they engage in all that talk. Second, talking is noisy, something we may find embarrassing. As teachers, we are always concerned about what the teacher next door, the vice-principal in the hallway, or the parent who shows up unannounced is thinking when the classroom clamor is peaking. We hear the comments: *Surely those students are just playing! Are they just having fun in there? Well then, they can't be learning!* Third, talk is considered difficult to assess. Unlike a paper-and-pencil test, it must be assessed as it occurs, *on the run.* So, we have the control consideration, the noise issue, and the assessment factor to address. The three things are interconnected.

To deal with the issues of teacher control, classroom noise, and effective ongoing assessment, it helps to continually remind ourselves of the many benefits and joys of real talk and real discussions in our classrooms. First, though, let's consider these issues further.

## The Control Consideration

Creating a space where students are empowered to construct their own meanings and understandings through talk means cultivating a collaborative classroom community for the sharing of ideas. Doing this may seem risky, as it requires teachers to act not as lesson controllers, but as catalysts for learning. In a truly collaborative classroom, students will risk offering opinions instead of worrying about giving *right answers*. Where does one begin?

Knowing how and when to give up some control and how to set up students to talk in order to learn is based partly on knowing how to assess student talk through ongoing observation and careful listening. We can then use our assessment to inform how we choose to guide further learning, including learning how to engage in good discussions. We can use our assessment information to judge what and how to model better oral communication and discussion techniques, for example, and thereby address issues such as excessive noise and off-topic chatter.

## The Noise Issue

When students are fully engaged in conversing and discussing with one another, there will be emphatic, even passionate voices, multiple points of view with arguments and disagreements, as well as plenty of laughter. In other words, there will be noise. We *want* our students to think, challenge, criticize, and develop alternative perspectives while expressing their ideas with vigor. This requires a free, but safe social environment.

This chapter considers the characteristics of what Cazden (2001) termed *real discussions* and looks at the teacher's role in engaging in this kind of discourse and creating conditions where it can flourish. Real discussions fall under the umbrella term *real talk* (Boyd & Galda, 2011), which is unscripted, flexible, and guided by students' expression of their ideas, connections, and understandings. Teacher guidance helps to extend, not control, those understandings. The teacher's role is to serve as purposeful planner and artistic director of student talk in the classroom.

Integral to dealing with *excessive* noise is the use of effective strategies to ensure that group discussions are conducted in a fair and courteous manner — what can be labeled ethical, or good, talk. Guidelines for good talk among students should be set clearly. (Strategies for achieving it, along with an anchor chart, are provided on pages 23 to 27.)

## The Assessment Factor

The vision for this chapter calls for teachers really talking with and listening to their students, and striving to know them in all their diversity. Achieving this is essential for fair assessment and for a healthy learning environment. We need to really listen to find out what our students are thinking and feeling, and to discover how and what they are learning and want to learn. This kind of communication with students is what constitutes real discussion (Cazden, 2001).

Engaging in real discussions with our students contributes to making connections and creating a community of learners. In our role as teachers, we are also responsible for creating conditions where students can grow and improve as communicators. Where do we begin? Let's begin with the importance of having real discussions as part of our assessment of student talk.

## Having Real Discussions with Our Students

When we talk to or with our students, are we *really conversing*, or *discussing*, or are we engaging in formal classroom talk, or *recitation*? (Cazden, 1988, 2001). Let's clarify the distinction:

| Classroom Talk as "real discussion" | Classroom Talk as "recitation" |
| --- | --- |
| What time is it, Sarah? | What time is it, Sarah? |
| Half-past two. | Half-past two. |
| Thanks. | Right. |
| (Cazden, 1988, pp. 30–31) | |

In the above illustration, the sequence on the right is a three-turn, teacher-dominated pattern. The teacher Initiates with a question, a student Responds, and the teacher Evaluates that response. This is called an "IRE sequence." The IRE sequence is criticized by Cazden as the most common default pattern in teacher-led exchanges, unlikely to change unless "deliberate action is taken to achieve some alternative" (2001, p. 53).

### Two Images of Teacher Talk

Research on teacher talk (e.g., Alvermann, O'Brien, & Dillon, 1990; Edwards & Westgate, 1994) indicates a discrepancy between teacher belief and practice: teachers believe in discussion as a forum for open exchange and yet they set the questions, use student answers to evaluate recall of facts, and insist on students raising their hands. In these formal classroom exchanges, we have "the image of the teacher as an orchestrator of the interactions, conducting the responses from the class, signaling who should contribute and controlling the outcomes" (Myhill, Jones, & Hopper, 2006, p. 14).

Contrasting with this image, consider the following.

Vivian Paley recorded conversations in her Kindergarten class where *real discussion* flourished. The class had been reading, discussing, and doing art and drama based on books by Leo Lionni. Here is a (paraphrased) conversation that occurred during their third or fourth reading of Lionni's *Alexander and the Wind-up Mouse*:

**When the Teacher Is a Conductor**

If students have to raise their hands and be acknowledged by the teacher before they can speak, then they are really addressing the teacher, not their peers.

REENY: That reminds me. Is Willy a boy?
  *They look together through the book, and the Teacher reads,* "One day Willy told a strange story. 'I've heard,' *he whispered mysteriously . . .*"
REENY: Then he is a boy. So why is they all mostly boys?
TEACHER: In the Leo Lionni books? Are they?
  *The children bring the entire collection to the rug.*
TEACHER: I've never thought about this before. Reeny says the characters are all boys. Let's see if it is so.
  *She holds up each book in turn.* Tico?
CHILDREN: A boy!
TEACHER: Swimmy?
CHILDREN: A boy!
TEACHER: Frederick, Cornelius, Pezzettino?
CHILDREN: All boys!
WALTER (*to Reeny*): Girls could be too. Swimmy you was too.
TEACHER: Walter is right. You were Swimmy and Frederick and Pezzenttino too. We've been acting out all these books without thinking about boys or girls.
REENY: That's because we do it all together. But when I was Swimmy all by myself I thought about it. Swimmy should be a girl.
(*Based on Paley, 1997, pp. 68–69*)

Several things are noteworthy about this discussion. First, it is a student, not the teacher, who poses the initial question. Second, the teacher engages *with* the students as they discuss the opening question. Third, the teacher provides the time and space (on the rug), as well as the concrete resources (the Lionni collection) that make the discussion possible. Finally, it is a student who draws conclusions and has the last word — we do not hear the teacher saying "right" or "correct." The teacher was really listening and thinking about the student's question and the other students' thoughts and opinions.

The teacher was not caught up in her own thoughts about the discussion, but was, instead, focused on the students' thoughts. When she did interject her own thinking, she did it in a conversational way, not in an evaluative way: "I've never thought about this before."

How can we ensure that we have *real discussions* such as Vivian Paley had with her students, where our students are equal collaborators with us in creating the conversation? By participating in dialogue, that is, by listening and speaking in response to what the students are saying — and by not dominating the discussion — we can make *real talk* possible. In addition, we can model how not to hold unfair power over the other participants.

## Towards Students Holding Real Discussions of Their Own

And how can we take this one step further? How can we guide our students to participate in a similar way when discussing a question or topic?

Eventually, we want our students to be as independent as possible, holding real discussions of their own. There are practical as well as pedagogical reasons for this. Sometimes, we are unavailable, for example, and as time goes on, we hope to gradually release responsibility, offering less support and allowing students to self-regulate. How can our students learn to engage effectively in real talk with less intervention from us? How can they learn how to conduct fair, truly collaborative conversations where every group member feels free to contribute? Further, how can we encourage talk that is truly a medium for learning: talk that promotes critical and creative thinking?

Many — perhaps most — students do not arrive in our classrooms knowing how to participate effectively and fairly in partner or group discussions. Discussions are social events mediated by ethical considerations such as courtesy and fairness. It is up to us to provide appropriate modelling and guidance.

## On the Need for a "Good Talk" Model

The term *accountable talk* refers to talk that is meaningful, respectful, and mutually beneficial to both speaker and listener (Allen, 2002). Here, however, we will use the term *good talk*, but it will include Allen's sense of talk that is accountable. The word *accountable* implies actions that are possibly liable or blameworthy — young students are not likely to make much sense of it. The word *good* implies a much broader spectrum of actions, including actions that are done well, but are also worthy, valued, and wholesome in the moral or ethical sense. Since talk is essentially a social activity, behavioral norms and ethical considerations are relevant.

To provide an example: The 2004 study by Almasi and colleagues found that power struggles ensued when new students who were unfamiliar with the norms of peer discussion joined the classroom. This pattern was especially evident to the researchers when the new students were of a lower social class. It points to the importance of teachers learning how to encourage classroom talk that is fair and equitable.

## Strategies for Cultivating Good Talk

Plan to teach your students how to have a good discussion. Aim for dynamic, but respectful interactions. Explicit instruction in how to engage in good talk can be provided through teacher modelling and time for discussion practice in small groups followed by feedback.

**Informal debates:** One strategy is to use mock debates where students practise respectfully disagreeing with one another. First, though, model what this sounds like and looks like, either working with a student or having two students model. For example, you could model listening attentively while making eye contact with the speaker, and adopt a sample statement starter such as "Yes, but I have a different idea …"

Here are more sentence frames to support communication goals:

- *how to disagree courteously, but clearly:* I disagree with . . . because . . .
- *how to present one's own ideas effectively:* My theory is . . . because . . .
- *how to encourage quiet group members:* Jay, what do you think about . . . ? How do you feel about . . . ?
- *how to build on one another's ideas by responding with AND statements:* Teacher example: "I noticed how you built on one another's ideas. When Jay said, 'It was cool when Henry Finch got the beast to let him go,' Melissa said, '*And* it was interesting that he was talking to the beast inside his head!' When

we add to the conversation with AND statements, it keeps the conversation going."

These sentence frames can be taught and discussed during Community Circle and then posted in the classroom for reference. Point out that some of them can be used during debates — for example, how to disagree courteously and how to present your own ideas effectively. Others can be applied to any group discussion.

Emphasize the *practice* of debating rather than the winning of a debate. Divide the class into pros and cons by having students number themselves off as 1 or 2. All the 1s are to argue pro; all the 2s are to argue con. This approach ensures that some students will have to argue for a side they may not agree with. Possible topics for brief debates include these:

- Was Frederick avoiding work when he gathered words and colors while the other mice were gathering food?
- Should recess be cancelled when it is raining outside?
- Should the Toronto Maple Leafs have won the hockey game last night?
- Should bus drivers be allowed to kick unruly passengers off their buses?

**Role-plays:** Another strategy is to use role-plays to practise each of the criteria, such as speaking politely. When first introducing guidelines, you may want to divide the class into groups of four, with one guideline assigned per group. Each group rehearses a brief role-play (no more than eight lines), to demonstrate their guideline. Once groups have practised, they can present to the whole class and students can debrief.

When students are familiar with the guidelines, they may need reminding if you (or they) notice that some partner or group discussions have not been models of good talk. It may be useful to present brief illustrations, on an as-needed basis, of one or two of the criteria just before a large-group, small-group, or partner discussion. For example, you may want a demonstration of how to disagree politely. You could direct two students to stand up to discuss snack foods, saying one likes chips but the other calls them junk and prefers fruit. Once the students have held their impromptu debate, the rest of the students could discuss what they did well and how they might improve.

Common criteria are listed on the anchor chart "Guidelines for Good Talk," on page 27. Embedding good talk in daily discussions and conversations is another approach. As she explains, Michelle does this in her classroom through Community Circle.

## The Real Question: Michelle

My approach is to reinforce *good talk* or *good conversational practices* during and through the daily Community Circle. That way, I am continually coaching what is expected. I am constantly reinforcing effective and respectful oral communication. It is part of our everyday practice because it is the ritual that begins each day. I model and comment on talking and listening behavior, including courtesy, knowing when to speak, knowing how and when to apologize, knowing when to say more, when to say less, and so on.

This is an explicit focus at the beginning of the year, but through daily practice, the students catch on and begin to regulate their own participation. In this way, when they are discussing a topic in the group, the focus is on what they are thinking and saying about a question or quotation, for example — it's not on the rules or norms. I do use self-assessment criteria, which are posted in the room, but once the guidelines are internalized, the students are free to think and communicate their thinking. In other words, talking and thinking about *talk* is not the final goal. Self-assessment is a means to an end, that is, better talk for higher-level thinking and learning. The real question is, *What are students learning from this discussion?*

## Inspiring and Supporting Student Talk

**Make use of task cards.** Organizational aids, such as anchor charts, graphic organizers, and task cards, can be used to focus and track discussion. Michelle makes great use of task cards with focus questions, quotations, and role-playing instructions. The cards for discussion vary with the current classroom focus. Some of the questions are specific to a text the class has read, while others may be more generally applicable.

After reading *Hana's Suitcase*, for example, Michelle read the card with this rich question to guide the discussion:

Hana wanted to be a teacher. Did she become a teacher? In what sense?

*Hana's Suitcase*, by Karen Levine, is part of the Holocaust Remembrance Series for Young Readers. It tells the story of Hana Brady's suitcase, which was sent to Japan from the Auschwitz museum, and then made its way to Canada, where Hana's brother was found alive. Hana's writing, found in the suitcase, told readers about what kind of girl Hana was and revealed that she had dreamed of being a teacher before becoming a victim of the Holocaust. The suitcase toured the world and became the focus of a documentary film. Prompted by the question, Michelle's students discussed in groups of four how Hana realized her dream after her death because of the "teachings" in her suitcase.

As another example, after reading *The Dot* by Peter Reynolds, Michelle provided the card shown at the top of the next page to stimulate discussion:

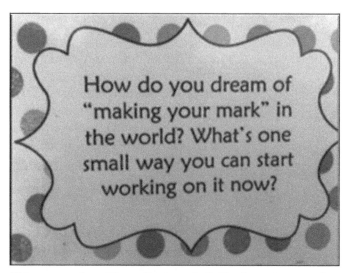

*This same card readily applies to an individual wanting to make a difference. It can be used with* Terry Fox: A Story of Hope *by Maxine Trottier,* A Picture Book of Martin Luther King, Jr. *by David A. Adler, and* I Am Rosa Parks *by Rosa Parks.*

In Michelle's class, the card prompted students to voice ideas like these:

- "My dream of making my mark is to join Rotary for Kids and help raise money and give the poor the money they need to get food and water. I want to travel around the world to help the poor. First step is to find a way to raise money!" (Cali, Grade 4)
- "My dream is to entertain for those who need it the most, like when they are sad, and to be in a show. I will make this happen by daydreaming and thinking about what you want to do when you are older." (Sofi, Grade 3)
- "My dream of making a mark is to help animals. I can start by awareness by saying animals are friends, not food. I can also help out at the SPCA (Humane Society)." (Tanya, Grade 4)
- "I want to make my mark by being helpful. Being nice by standing up for others. One small way is to stay after class and help clean up." (Jay, Grade 4)

At other times, Michelle uses cards to present an array of social dilemmas for her students to talk about. Dilemmas are based on possible everyday situations. Here is the text of two task cards used by Michelle:

> You see your best friend playing with someone else. What do you do?
>
> If you do something embarrassing, what can you do to keep your problem small?

Depending on the time of year and what else the class is involved in, the cycle of discussion topics is changed. Each day a student selects one card from a small bag, and then the talking stone is passed along for each student to offer opinions.

**Promote respectful talk.** Whether during whole-group, small-group, or partner talk, Michelle does not tolerate inappropriate comments; instead, she guides and models:

"I guide students on how to disagree using respectful language, how to build on each other's ideas, and how to encourage all their group members to participate. I also model how to enter appropriately or 'interrupt politely' into free-flowing discussions and conversations.

"I model and teach appropriate voice volume for classroom talk. I explain that we need a noise level that allows us all to hear what others are saying. I use very flexible seating arrangements so that students can sit in a circle, at a small table, or on cushions in the corner. I allow pairs, trios, and small groups, formed by the students themselves. This increases student participation and responsibility. At times, I have to remind them to include someone who may be left out. We practise these things regularly throughout the year."

**Engage students in creating an anchor chart.** Review success criteria and self-assessment criteria. Co-construct an anchor chart on good talk with your students. Invite students to contribute to the rules. The chart could be as simple as the statement *When I am listening, my eyes are looking at the speaker, my mouth is closed, and my hands are still.* Post the chart in the classroom. A sample anchor chart is outlined below.

---

### Guidelines for Good Talk

**Speak** politely. Say please and thank you, use your classmates' names, and speak at medium volume.

**Listen** attentively. Make eye contact, keep an open mind, and show an open heart.

**Focus** on the topic or purpose of the discussion.

**Respond** with questions or comments that build on each other's ideas.

**Back up** your opinions with good reasons or evidence from the text.

**Share responsibility for the group:** take turns, stay on topic, and be positive and encouraging.

---

## Assessing Talk: Part of Purposeful Planning

As noted earlier in this chapter, teacher assessment of talk can be challenging. Although students should be guided to assess their own participation in speaking and listening activities, as teachers we are accountable on another level. When it comes to documenting growth in oral communication skills, what are the best assessment practices?

### The Lens of Pedagogical Documentation

Really discussing with our students, particularly when we listen attentively, can contribute to that form of assessment referred to as *pedagogical documentation*. This way of assessing reflects the ways in which teachers "learn *with* their students in collaborative, social contexts, and go beyond traditional evidence-gathering, such as paper and pencil tasks, to better understand how students learn through play, inquiry projects, conversations, and social interactions" (Campbell, Brownlee, & Renton, 2016, p. 1).

With this kind of assessment lens, the primary purpose is not to interrogate or judge; rather, the idea is to value the learners' own perspectives on their learning. In the case of oral communication development, we can then take steps to create conditions whereby our students can become more articulate communicators. Kindergarten teacher Carole Anne Renton says this about using pedagogical documentation: "I come to know my students on a much deeper level, making differentiated instruction easier to achieve. I watch in awe as young children grow into strong, capable learners accustomed to sharing their thinking in open dialogue with peers and teachers."

Emergent and struggling speakers, readers, and writers, including English language learners, require the use of finely tuned instruction and effective strategies to enhance their oral language proficiency. They also require diverse opportunities to talk and be listened to, and multiple opportunities for feedback and response. Careful assessment is critical in the development of oral language, particularly with those who are learning English as a second language or for those whose oral language development requires more time and practice.

The questions we need to ask are these:

- How can we really listen to our students?
- How can they feel truly free to express themselves and not feel that the goal is to come up with the "right" answer?
- How can we encourage them to articulate their thoughts, feelings, and learning stories every day?
- How can we best document and follow up on these learning stories so that the stories have the greatest potential to cultivate strong communication skills and improve student learning and well-being?

## Two Key Processes in Assessment of Oral Communication

By *learning story*, we mean documentation, captured in words and pictures, of an event (or series of events), such as a milestone or a breakthrough in understanding, showing how an individual demonstrated learning.

Assessment in order to help students become articulate communicators encompasses both assessment *for* learning and assessment *as* learning. As part of assessment *for* learning, teachers provide students with *descriptive feedback* and *coaching* for improvement. Being able to do this depends on observing and listening closely. Teachers engage in assessment *as* learning by providing tasks and activities that allow students to develop into independent learners; in other words, students should be able to set individual goals, monitor their progress, determine next steps, and reflect on their thinking and learning (Ontario Ministry of Education, 2010, p. 28). As an example, after reading a common text, students could set up their own small-group discussion, create the questions and topics for it, assess their own participation and the quality of their discussion as individuals and as a group, and then reflect on how they might improve next time.

We can ensure that learning is made visible and audible by listening to student discussions and learning stories, and by keeping good records. Assessment information about oral communication proficiency can be obtained and documented in the same way as most learning, that is, through formal and informal observations. We can keep records of conversations and discussions by video or audio taping, and by making ongoing anecdotal notes. As we document student learning, we will discover how to provide timely and meaningful feedback and guidance. Documenting all comes down to *attentive listening*, followed by reflection on what kind of learning was taking place and how that learning can be extended.

As for the students, talking about their learning experiences is part of the learning process. As students articulate their learning stories for their peers and for their teacher, they become aware of what and how they have learned at a metacognitive level.

Two key processes are involved in assessing oral communication effectively: (1) listening attentively; and (2) providing feedback and coaching in ways that make sense to students. In other words, *we* must be articulate communicators if we are to model effective language use and provide helpful coaching and guidance. Doing this entails having real discussions with our students.

### Teacher Involvement: How Much? How Little?

Research on effective peer discussion (Almasi et al., 2004; Maloch, 2002; McIntyre, 2007; Wells, 1999) indicates that student talk is most successful when teachers provide strategic scaffolding. For example, Maloch's (2002) research showed how a teacher's modelling, the way she asked pertinent follow-up questions, and how she highlighted what students did well in their discussions effectively supported student talk. This was demonstrated by the students' immediate use of these strategies in the next conversation.

On the other hand, knowing when to step back and allow the students to problem-solve is important. Here's how Michelle puts it:

"We need to navigate the process together. The learning happens in the struggle. Don't run to the rescue right away! Keep your ears open for the right time to ask a question to focus their thinking and talk, for example. Providing rich tasks and rich topics for discussion is like providing a good meal. My classroom is not like a five-star restaurant with the kind of French service where waiters are hovering and ready to step in at every bite. I believe in offering a great meal, but letting them enjoy it! Wait and see, and be there only when really needed. I hold back until my contribution can add just the right spice at the right moment."

## Conditions for Creating a Classroom Where Talk Flourishes

There are powerful interconnections between the development of oral language and of literacy in general. The fact that oral language is learned in use, in a variety of real-life contexts, and under identifiable learning conditions informs our teaching of literacy. We also know that the same neural machinery used for oral language is also used in literacy activities. It therefore makes sense to promote growth in listening and speaking skills in the classroom literacy program from the early years and beyond to build the necessary foundations for literacy learning.

Cambourne's (2000/2001) model of learning includes these key conditions for learning how to talk and for becoming literate:

- immersion in resources and opportunities for practice — lots of talk, plenty of texts
- demonstration or expert modelling of the ability (talking or reading) to be acquired
- expectations on the part of those with whom the learner is bonded that the learner will achieve or succeed (These expectations are understood implicitly in the early years and should be explicitly discussed in formal contexts.)
- responsibility for decision making on the part of the learners about what, when, and how to learn
- responses consisting of relevant, timely, and appropriate feedback from knowledgeable others
- employment of the time and opportunity to practise what is being learned in functional, authentic ways (Diverse groupings, such as whole group, partner, and trio, are essential here to maximize student participation.)

- approximations, or the freedom to make mistakes as the desired model is approached

Finally, *engagement* is the key condition throughout all the above conditions: it is the guiding principle when choosing effective oral language strategies.

Emergent and struggling or *striving* speakers, readers, and writers, including English language learners, require many rich opportunities and effective strategies to make progress as oral language communicators. They require engagement in diverse activities where they can talk and be listened to, with ongoing feedback and response. Cambourne's model shows us the critical conditions we must create in our classrooms, particularly for those whose oral language development requires more time and practice. The talk strategies presented in this book have been chosen with Cambourne's conditions in mind.

## The Last Word: Students Talk About Talk

As teachers, we all want our students to understand the value and purpose of talk. To check the understanding of some students, we invited five Grade 3 or 4 students to comment on the Rubin quotation that introduced this chapter: "Talk is like the sea." We asked, "What would you say talk is like?"

LUCY: Talk is like music. Your mouth is an instrument.
ALI: YES! You're expressing the song of your emotions . . . Talk is like food. Once you've had it, though, it's gone. You can't have the exact same conversation twice. You can talk to different people about the same thing, but it's a different conversation. Just like sharing different meals with different people.
SADI: Yes, I'll add to what Ali said. Talk is like pasta, you know? (*laughing*) 'Cause you're stirring it around in the pot, or you twirl it on your fork, and it's like you've got an interesting twist to your conversation.
JAY (*after thinking a long time*): Talking is like walking. You can move around, walk around, and you don't always know where you might end up.

We then asked the students to comment on the importance of *listening*, and some of them continued to think metaphorically:

CALI: Listening is like a circle, 'cause you're always listening. It never really stops. It reminds me of a TV show character, Garnet. She hardly ever talks, 'cause she's always listening. And that makes her strong.
ALI: Listening is like the world. Listening adds to your reality. Without listening, you wouldn't know how to do new things, how to understand things. Without listening in the classroom, for instance, it would be straight off chaos —nobody would know what to do. And without that, no one would learn.
JAY: That's right. Listening helps you learn. You learn from other people by listening to them. Listening to the teacher helps you learn. If you didn't listen, you wouldn't know what to do; you wouldn't understand. You just wouldn't learn. And if you didn't learn, you wouldn't know anything.

The next chapter explores specific oral language strategies designed for student participation in purposeful conversations and discussions.

# 3

## Learning Out Loud: Talk Strategies for Students

*Classroom talk provides all participants with opportunities to learn and talk together, and thus to tap into the social and cognitive functions of language.*

— *Maureen Boyd and Lee Galda, 2011, p. 3*

 *Talking helps me learn, 'cause I can explain my thinking, and it's way easier than explaining in writing.*

— *Chris, Grade 3 student*

This chapter focuses on key strategies you can use to get students really talking and thinking. It builds on Chapter 2, where the focus was on how you as a teacher play a central role in creating the conditions for lively and constructive classroom talk, thereby developing a dialogic classroom. Here, the goal is to present enjoyable speaking and listening strategies that contribute to the development of your students as articulate communicators.

This chapter includes a selection of whole-group, small-group, and partner discussion strategies that we have found best promote higher-level engagement and critical thinking. It highlights two specific strategies in detail based on experiences in Michelle's Grade 3–4 classroom. The first strategy is called Sketch to Stretch *Plus*, based on Harste and Burke's (1988) original post-reading strategy, with additional time for small-group discussion and whole-group sharing. Next, we present a strategy which could be called Working with Wordless Books. Wordless books are viewed, discussed at two levels, and then produced by the students.

Finally, we describe several effective partner, small-group, and whole-group talk strategies used by Michelle in her classrooms and by Terry with her teacher candidates.

### Sketch to Stretch *Plus*

*Sequence:* Read (listen to, view a text presented), talk, sketch, discuss drawings in small group, and then share with the whole class.

This version of Harste and Burke's (1988) post-reading strategy gives more time for small-group discussion and whole-group sharing; it also includes the option of adding words and graphics to the sketches. The original concept is to invite students to *sketch* their responses to a story, usually one that has been read aloud, without worrying about creating a work of art. The goal is to *stretch* their thinking, since the act of drawing often sparks a deeper discussion of the story. Using talk and drawing together is an evidence-based practice recognizing that children's drawings communicate thought (Eisner, 2002) and that drawing, talking, reading, and writing are all neurologically connected as learning processes (Cambourne, 2017).

The important thing is to stretch one's level of meaning making in response to a story and to express personal connections symbolically and orally. Before beginning their drawings, the students are given the opportunity to discuss their immediate reactions to the story. They then create individual sketches, and when the small group is ready, members discuss their drawings. By producing a sketch, however simple, each student has an opportunity to tap into individual thoughts and feelings, and is then able to bring something both concrete and symbolic to the table to talk about. The process of drawing seems to release words that students may not have found easy to express.

Michelle has found that this strategy is suitable for all students, but particularly for those whose thinking abilities are well beyond what they are able to write, for whatever reason. "The students who benefit most from Sketch to Stretch might have a specific learning disability, or maybe they are just not there yet developmentally, or English may be a second or third language," she says. "Whatever the reason, drawing and talking can allow them to express sophisticated ideas. They also enjoy listening to one another talk about their interpretations. There is a deeper level of understanding and empathy for one another that develops. Plus, during the sharing time, there is always lots of laughter. The students often spontaneously nominate one another to share during the whole-group discussion. For example: 'Liam, share yours. It's really good!'"

The sketches represent something the story meant personally to the students. They can be as simple as a symbol or color. For example, in response to a story where love conquers all, the student may sketch a single red heart above a drawing of Earth. In response to *How to Catch a Star* by Oliver Jeffers, one student drew the sketch shown below. It does not represent anything actually in the story, but as she said, "My drawing shows how I would feel if I could catch a star; that is, it would be awesome! I would feel happy, like a dream come true!" The students in her group knew exactly how she felt when they saw her sketch and listened to her explanation.

*What it might feel like to catch a star*

Other students may choose to depict a specific scene or episode that stood out for them. At first, this may seem to demonstrate literal-level comprehension, but when the students discuss their drawings, deeper levels of meaning will surface. For example, after listening to Eve Bunting's *Smoky Night*, one student said,

> I just couldn't stop thinking about those firefighters saving the cats from the burning . . . I was so worried about the cats, and they got them out. I wish I could be brave like that! When the teacher read the story and showed the pictures, I felt like I was really there. And I like the way the pictures from the book looked, so I tried to draw a little like the illustrator.

*This sketch shows the student's concern about cats being rescued from fire in a style somewhat like that of book illustrator David Diaz.*

## The Strategy Applied to *The Crow's Tale*

Stories that include dramatic events, clear characters, and personal or emotional messages tend to stimulate drawing and talking most effectively. In Michelle's Grade 3–4 class, we read aloud *The Crow's Tale*, based on the Lenni Lenape legend, retold by Naomi Howarth in rhyming verse.

The tale recounts how Crow risks its life by flying up to the Sun to bring fire to the freezing animals below. Crow begins its journey with rainbow-colored feathers and a beautiful singing voice, but returns in scorched blackness with a croaky voice, triumphantly carrying the burning branch back to the animals. Although Crow is saddened by the loss of its beauty, the Sun points out that it is still beautiful with its iridescent feathers and brave character.

### The Read-Aloud

Terry introduced *The Crow's Tale* by telling the students that the book recounts an Indigenous North American legend, this version from the Lenape people. She said that similar legends are told by the Ojibwe people. David Bouchard, for example, tells the Ojibwe version in another beautiful book, *Rainbow Crow*. This much longer book was showed to the students and made available to them for later comparison.

Sitting in circle formation, the students listened intently to the dramatic story and were given plenty of time to view the illustrations. They were captivated by the illustrations, especially the final one depicting the crow's shimmering feathers.

## Sketching After the Read-Aloud

Before students began making their sketches, we had a brief talk about the main message of the story. Here is what some of the students said:

- "It doesn't matter if people think you are ugly; it matters if you are beautiful on the inside."
- "Crow was brave. He was selfless. He could have been burnt up by the Sun."
- "He took a big risk for the other animals."

Michelle then quickly reviewed what Sketch to Stretch involves (they had all engaged in the strategy previously). Michelle told them: "Make a *sketch*. It does not have to be an artistic drawing. It should be a drawing about your own thoughts and feelings based on the story and what it means to you. Think about what is important to you about this story and how you can draw that. You can also add a few words if that helps you express what's important." She also reminded them to draw quietly and to be ready to talk about their drawings and thinking with their table group or partner. "After that, we can share with everybody."

Most students sat quietly thinking before putting pencil to paper. Some used regular pencils, and others chose to use pencil crayons. Some spoke quietly to their neighbors, but most drew in silence until they were ready to discuss their drawings. Some students added captions below their drawings, but what they said orally was always more detailed and involved.

## Partner Chat

The *Plus* in Sketch to Stretch is all the talking that students do in partner, small-group, and large-group formations after the read-aloud and after they finish their sketches. Encouragement to add words to their drawings is also part of this.

Here are several samples of what students shared about their drawings with their partners:

*A.*

These are the two most important things in the story. I drew a rainbow, for the colors of the crow at the beginning, and then I drew a black crow feather, 'cause that's what Crow turned into after, and that's what crows have now.

[The drawing shows a simple rainbow on the left and a single black crow feather on the right.]

*B.*

This is the part where the owl said, Who will go to the sun? See, here are the animals who couldn't go 'cause they can't fly: polar bear, rabbit, seal, and deer, and here is the owl in the tree. See, it had to be the crow who had to go.

[The drawing shows the animals in silhouette form, facing the owl in a leafless tree.]

*C.*

See, this is Crow after it came back. But it's not black in my drawing 'cause I'm drawing how it looks on the inside. I think it doesn't matter what you look like; it's how your attitude is. And the crow still had beauty inside him, but it was just under all of the black burnt stuff.

[The drawing shows Crow with a bright yellow body and brilliantly colored wings — red, orange, yellow, green, blue, and purple.]

*D.*

I felt bad for the crow when it came back and cried. But the wind blew the clouds away so the sun could come out. That's when the sun told the crow, "You are selfless and brave. Can you not see what others can see? You are as beautiful as you could possibly be."

[The drawing of Crow crying is featured below.]

*E.*

My picture shows before and after the crow went to the sun. He gave the ultimate sacrifice of his beauty for everybody else. His most beautiful rainbow feathers, all burnt and black because he brought back the burning branch. What he did was selfless. He sacrificed his beauty. But he was still beautiful on the inside. It's like if I went into a fire and came back with all black, and my hair all rough and crispy and burnt.

[The before-and-after drawing featured at the top of the next page here lacks the color "before," but still conveys some of the changes Crow underwent.]

In one small-group discussion, three students talked about the fact that the story did not say whether Crow was a girl or a boy. They referred to the book to make sure of this fact. During the whole-group discussion, one of the students said:

> It doesn't matter if you're a girl or a boy. It doesn't matter if you're big or small. The owl is saying, "Someone had to do it" and it doesn't matter about boy-girl, big small, whatever. It matters what's inside of you. And you should be selfless. That's what matters.

[This sketch of Crow setting out on its quest includes speech bubbles emphasizing the owl's words.]

## Discussing the Use of Poetry

Finally, prompted by us, the students discussed the author's decision to use rhyming verse to tell *The Crow's Tale*.

MICHELLE: I love music, and poetry is like music. It has rhythm and beat, so I really like the poetry in this book. Mrs. Campbell sings in a choir, so I think she must like songs.

TERRY: Yes, and the words in this book are like a song. Not all poetry rhymes, but in this book we have rhyming poetry, like a song.

STUDENTS (sample musings):
- "The poetry makes the story more meaningful."
- "It sounds more exciting."
- "It's not like ordinary language — the story would just be ordinary without the poetry."
- "The poetry matched the pictures better."

MICHELLE: Ahh, you mean the pictures were poetic?

STUDENT: Yes, beautiful pictures, beautiful words.

## Determining What Goes on the Quotation Wall

To wrap up this session with *The Crow's Tale*, the students were asked which words from the book stood out the most for them. After much discussion, they reached a consensus on the following quotations, found near the end of the story after Crow, sad and feeling unlovable, returns with burnt feathers and a croaky voice. Both are spoken by the Sun. These quotations were printed on chart paper and posted on the class's quotation wall for students to refer to and ponder.

> "Dear Crow," said the Sun, "you are selfless and brave.
> It is not how you look, but how you behave.
> Can you not see what the others can see?
> You're as beautiful as you could possibly be."

> Pretty or ugly, slim, thin or fatter
> your beauty inside is the heart of the matter.

Collaboratively choosing a memorable quotation is a regular practice in Michelle's class. The posted quotation is one that makes students think and wonder. As Michelle puts it:

"This is *meaning making*. Every day. One or more students 'nominate' a quote. We highlight it on the Smart Board. The nominators defend their choice. We all discuss it, and if there is a general consensus, we post that quote and come back to it whenever there is a new connection."

Michelle first came to use a quotation wall while working with Jon Muth's *The Three Questions* (based on the Tolstoy tale). The students engaged in a graffiti activity. Three large pieces of butcher paper were set out on tables with the three questions from the book:

> When is the best time to do things?
>
> Who is the most important one?
>
> What is the right thing to do?"

The students wrote their ideas on one paper and then moved to the next, with Michelle playing a song as a signal to move on. When the students ended up at their original paper, they looked at the recorded thoughts of their peers. They then summarized what was on their paper. The class held a grand conversation on the topic as a whole. The students then came up with a single saying to answer each question.

The time is now.

You, with me now, are the most important one.

Kindness is the right thing to do.

These were the first statements posted on the wall. Since then, Michelle and her students consider a quotation a day. They discuss it, write what it means in their own words, talk about it as a class, and assess whether the words — two quotations in the case of *The Crow's Tale* — are worth posting on the wall. Michelle says, "I don't change the quotes; we just add to them. I never planned the quotation wall — it just happened!"

### Possible Extension Activities for *The Crow's Tale*

- Students in Grades 5 to 8 could compare *The Crow's Tale* to longer versions of the legend. For example, there is *Rainbow Crow* by Canadian Métis author David Bouchard, richly illustrated by David Jean; the book includes a CD in English and Ojibwe. In partner or small-group discussions, students could compare both the language and illustration styles through T-charts that include sketches and key words.
- One way to further explore Indigenous stories dealing with truth and bravery, beauty and ugliness, is to read aloud *The Rough-Face Girl* by Rafe Martin, illustrated by David Shannon, and have the class discuss the Algonquin legend.
- Both *The Crow's Tale* and *The Rough-Face Girl* lend themselves to either Readers theatre in small groups (see Chapter 8) or oral storytelling individually or in tandem with a partner (see Chapter 7).
- Students could compare *The Crow's Tale* to other myths and legends where an animal or character had to be heroic in order to help the group. Recommended stories include *The Name of the Tree*, a Bantu tale retold by Celia Barker Lottridge; and *The Legend of the Lady Slipper*, an Ojibwe tale retold by Lise Lunge-Larsen and illustrated by Andrea Arroyo.

## Working with Wordless Books

*Sequence:* Students view, discuss, tell the story, and produce wordless texts.

In this strategy, wordless books are used to stimulate discussion of story possibilities and story co-creation. Students are involved in viewing, discussing, telling the story, and producing wordless texts of their own.

Michelle introduced the strategy by asking her class what a wordless book is. Their answers included the following:

- "It's a book with no words, so you have to tell the story in your mind."
- "You have to read the pictures."
- "You have to imagine what the words are that match the pictures."
- "It's a book where the pictures tell the story — you have to really look!"

### Show the Book to the Whole Group

Using a YouTube version so that all students could clearly see the pictures, we showed *Journey* by Aaron Becker. The story depicts the adventures of a girl who travels through a doorway she draws with her own red marker into a land of wonder and surprising challenges. She succeeds in overcoming her obstacles, using her red marker to draw a boat, a flying carpet, and a hot air balloon. She shows courage, creativity, and kindness which is repaid.

During the viewing, the students spontaneously began interjecting opinions on what the girl might draw next with her red marker.

- "She's drawing a door."
- "It's going to be a red boat."
- "What is it now? AHH! A flying carpet!"

And more. They showed considerable focus.

At the end, after the girl had solved all the problems presented by drawing an appropriate object to get her out of trouble, the students applauded and said they really liked the story. Michelle asked, "What did you like about it?"

- "Every time she drew something new, it became a new story."
- "She went on an adventure."
- "She set the bird free, and the bird brought her red crayon back when she needed it to escape."
- "It always worked out, and you knew it would all work out in the end."
- "The red crayon drawings created her journey."
- "The music made you believe it would have a happy ending."
- "The music was from Charlie Brown — that story was like a journey, too!"

## Have Small Groups Discuss a Second Wordless Book

Provide a copy of the wordless book *Tuesday* by David Wiesner for each group of three or four students. Explain that they are going to look slowly at the pictures and tell the story by adding the words that aren't there. Read the title and the first dated page, and remind students to examine each page carefully and talk about what is happening.

In Michelle's class, students engaged in two levels of discussion.

*Level 1:* The groups looked quickly through the book and then went back to the beginning to inspect and discuss each visual. At this point, they spent time examining the details in each illustration and talking about what was going on in it. Each group made sure that every group member added his or her voice, as multiple interpretations were possible even at this initial level.

*Level 2:* Students then took a third turn through the book before co-constructing a story. Most groups decided they would take turns voicing the words for each page. Students spontaneously spent extra time on the opening and closing, trying to reach a consensus. For example, in one group of four boys, one boy wanted the words to be in poetic form. For the first page, he proposed: "Frogs can fly. Turtle shows fear." Next page: "Frogs flying, turtle hiding." He was unable to sustain it on following pages, though, and got voted down. The group went on to describe what was happening on each page using everyday language:

"Here a man is eating a sandwich for his bedtime snack. He sees the frogs flying
    by the window."
"One frog is waving, Hi!" [*laughter*]
"And the man is going 'WHOA. What's that?'"

And so on. This group chose to present their version of the story in the same colloquial language.

Other groups wove a story from the pictures, using more literary language. The first example below consists of excerpts from one group's oral responses to the first page of text "Tuesday evening, around eight."

*This night was not like any other night . . .*
*For it is a night when the frogs can fly on their lily pads. They go whirling and swirling, one upside down, another chasing a startled crow . . .*
*The flying frogs get distracted and accidentally fly into somebody's clothes . . .*
[The text shows a washing line.]
*The dog, we'll call him Rusty, saw a frightening sight . . .*
*The investigators were confused. I wonder what's happened here . . .*

The two examples below pertain to the closing text: "Next Tuesday, 7:58 p.m."

*It was an ordinary end of the day at the barn. Until . . .* [turn page]
Group in Unison: **There were flying pigs!**

*When pigs can fly . . . It's next Tuesday!*

## Students Produce Wordless Books

Having explored the stories offered by wordless books, students went on to produce a variety of wordless books using hand-made drawings, images from the Internet, and photos, as they chose. They also used Book Creator on their iPads to publish and share their stories. Story titles included "Next Wednesday" and "When Pigs Can Fly!"

# Discussion Strategies for Partners

The two featured strategies are Say Something and Inside-Outside Circle, but first some ideas on how to create partners and what sorts of questions partners could consider together are offered.

## How to Use Talk Partners Effectively

- Use random pairings. The students see this as fair, and they get a chance to talk with and listen to someone they may not normally interact with one on one. Ways to achieve this include drawing names from a hat, having two sets of craft sticks with same numbers for students to draw and match, and using dice at table groups (first two to throw same number become partners).
- Let students know ahead of time if they will be sharing with a larger group or the whole class.
- Pose open-ended questions which have no right or wrong answers; be sure to include inferential, evaluative, and synthesis questions.
  *Inferential:* How do you know that . . . ? What makes you think that?
  *Evaluative:* How do you feel about that? Why?
  *Synthesis:* Is there anything you would have done differently? Why?
- To further extend thinking, ask students how they arrived at their answers.

**More Partner Talk Questions**
- What is important to remember about this book?
- What surprised you about this book?
- What are one or two experiences from your own life that connect with the story?
- Why do you think people should [or should not] read this story?

*Possible follow-up:* Discuss, then write one or two statements about someone whose point of view is [or is not] represented in the story. Or, talk and write in role as a character, describing inner feelings or plans for the future.

## Say Something

Say Something (Beers, 2003) offers opportunities for students to engage in accountable talk and deepen their understanding through predicting, questioning, inferring, responding, and making connections.

### Method

**Sample Prompts**

Revising an earlier prediction:
*I supposed . . . might happen, but now I see something else is taking place . . .*
Clarifying something you may have misunderstood:
*I thought I understood why . . . But now I realize . . .*
Making an argument and revising it:
*My first argument was in favor of . . . but a different perspective might be . . .*

1. Prepare an anchor chart listing some prompts. See, for example, Beers (2003, p. 108) for sample sentence stem charts for predicting, inferring, and so on.
2. Direct students to find a partner and number themselves 1 or 2.
3. Read or provide an interesting, thought-provoking text for the students, in chunks of three to five paragraphs.
4. Ask students to choose a sentence starter from the anchor chart.
5. Provide think time for students to formulate their response.
6. Direct partner 1 to begin sharing. When partner 1 is finished, partner 2 begins.
7. Observe pairs in discussion. When talk has subsided, chunk the next section for them to read.

*(Adapted from Beers, 2003, pp. 105–110)*

## Inside-Outside Circle

Inside-Outside Circle is a very effective way to share learning in the content areas.

Inside-Outside Circle (see Bennett & Rolheiser, 2001) offers opportunities for students to engage in accountable, or *good*, talk and experience a variety of ideas and perspectives. Every student gets a chance to speak with and listen to different people. No time is spent waiting.

### Method

**Sample Questions**

- What would you do with $150 to celebrate your country's birthday?
- Name three things your parents do for you because they want to make you happy.
- How do you think Terry Fox felt when he had to stop his run across Canada? [Possible context: Reading *Terry Fox: A Story of Hope*]

1. Direct students to find a partner and number themselves 1 or 2.
2. Direct all partner 1s to stand in a circle facing out. Have all partner 2s stand facing their partner.
3. Pose a question and provide about 30 seconds of think time.
4. Have partner 1 share his or her answer or solution with partner 2 and then signal when finished by saying "Pass." Partner 2 paraphrases what partner 1 said and then adds a response, which partner 1 paraphrases to complete the turn.
5. Rotate the outside circle one person to the left or right.
6. Direct new partners to share responses or pose a new question. Repeat the process (steps 4 to 6).

# Small-Group Discussion Strategies

Featured strategies are Carousel and Place Mat. Carousel provides an opportunity for students to talk about books or other topics and listen to a wide range of opinions. Place Mat offers a focused, small-group approach to reaching a consensus on a topic.

## Carousel

This rotating discussion group strategy can be used to converse about any number of topics. Terry uses this strategy in the B.Ed. program for teacher candidates to compare illustrated children's texts, both fiction and nonfiction. The teacher candidates discuss whether the books demonstrate traits of high-quality children's literature. The strategy can also be employed with larger groups of elementary school students.

Students are directed to arrange themselves in seven groups. Each group discusses the book placed at their table, which has been matched with one of the seven traits. Each group has a different book. One person records a summary of the discussion. The summary will include a brief synopsis of the text, the main points discussed by the group, and whether the book exemplifies the quality they were investigating. For example, table 1 reads *Scaredy Squirrel* by Mélanie Watt, which is paired with the quality of appeal. Does the group feel that this text would be appealing to children? Why or why not?

At each table someone becomes the stay-at-home armchair expert on one of these seven aspects: (1) overall book appeal, (2) good, dramatic story, (3) vivid language, (4) richness of message, allowing multiple interpretations, (5) story true to life, (6) how moralistic the text is, or (7) how relevant the text is to the learners (is text accurate? factual?).

When carousel music plays, each table group, but not the experts, will travel around to the next table. The armchair expert instructs each visiting group about the quality of the book reviewed and leads a discussion about whether that book exemplifies the given trait. The armchair experts learn about the books from the other tables during final presentations. We end with a grand conversation on what constitutes a high-quality children's text. Below is a strategy summary such as students might receive on a card.

Carousel is also effective in the content areas as it allows students to demonstrate their understanding and share information.

---

**Carousel Strategy in Brief**

- Use this small-group strategy for rotating discussion groups on any topic.
- Each group starts with a specific focus.
- One person in the group records a summary of the discussion.
- On a signal, the group rotates to another table.
- One group member stays behind as the "armchair expert" and tells the new group all about their discussion.
- Groups rotate until they are back at their home table.
- Each group presents to the whole group for the benefit of the experts.

---

## Place Mat

Place Mat is a collaborative learning activity that gives students an opportunity to share their ideas and learn from one another in a small-group setting. It can be used when the goal is to reach a consensus.

*Method*

1. Decide on a question or topic for the students to address.

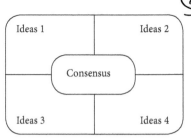

A template for four students using the Place Mat strategy

*Good idea*
*DLT strategy*

2. Organize the students into groups of four, and give each group a piece of chart paper or 11 by 17 paper.
3. Direct each group to draw a circle or square in the centre of the paper and then divide the remaining area of the paper into equal sections, with one section for each group member.
4. Ask the students to think about the chosen topic and then silently write about it in their own area of the paper for several minutes. Alternatively, they could use sticky notes for individual ideas and place them on a large chart-paper version of the place mat displayed for classroom viewing.
5. After several minutes, signal the students to stop. Direct them to discuss the ideas on the place mat with their group, looking for common elements. The group must reach a consensus and record the most important points in the centre of the place mat.
6. Each group shares its work with the other groups.

*(Adapted from Ontario Ministry of Education, 2003, p. 143)*

---

### Success Criteria for Self-Assessment of Collaborative Small-Group Discussions

A checklist like this one provides students with ideas on how to contribute effectively to discussions in small groups. Ideally, success criteria would be co-created with the students. They can be recorded on chart paper and posted for reference after a group discussion, laminated copies can be provided for each group and reused when appropriate, or paper copies can be distributed to the students so that they (as well as you) will have a record of their participation.

☐ I contributed my fair share to the discussion (not too much, not too little).
☐ I was prepared for the discussion. I thought about the text, had questions ready, and brought needed materials such as my Sketch to Stretch.
☐ I expressed my ideas clearly and supported them with reasons and evidence from the text.
☐ I listened carefully and respectfully, and made eye contact.
☐ I made comments or asked questions to ensure that I understood other students' ideas.
☐ I thought about and added to or extended other students' ideas in relevant ways.
☐ I made sure that I understood any point of view I disagreed with and backed up my view with reasons.
☐ I helped keep the discussion on topic.
☐ I helped keep the discussion fair for everyone.
☐ I took part in the large-group sharing after the discussion.
☐ I talked with the group about how to improve our discussions.

*(Adapted from Parr & Campbell, 2012, p. 48)*

# Whole-Group Discussions and Sharing

In this section we consider grand conversations and two ways of whole-group sharing: student-led book talks and Authors Share.

## Grand Conversations

Peterson and Eeds (1990) coined the term *grand conversations* as part of a literature-based reading program with the concept of story at the centre. They stress building community through reading aloud, as they see the grand conversation in terms of collaboration and dialogue (2007, p. 21). The focus of a grand conversation is interpretation of one text — ideally, a story — because awareness of literary elements is important. "Teachers of literature want children to be more than plot readers," Peterson and Eeds (2007, p. 26) assert.

An option is to use focusing questions for students who are unfamiliar with this form of discussion. Provide questions until students can formulate their own.

Whether fictional or informational texts are used, the primary goal of a grand conversation is to get students to move beyond the literal level and think and talk about the text by questioning and examining it from different points of view. Unlike literature circles, where students are sometimes assigned specific roles, there are no specific routines for grand conversations. They can occur in small groups or with the whole class. Ideally, they are student led and student directed, based on the authentic questions and issues the students wish to discuss together. The idea is to read and talk together about texts. In this way, grand conversations exemplify the type of talk described in Chapter 2 as *real discussions*, as opposed to teacher-dominated question-and-answer forms of discourse.

## Sharing: Focus on Individual Presentations

*Student-Led Book Talks:* Lucy Calkins (2001) wrote that the books that are most memorable and important to us are the ones we share and talk about with our friends and colleagues. Book talks provide this platform for our students so that they can share with their peers. A book talk is a brief, animated oral presentation of a book that a student has read. It is given to entice others to read the book.

Book talks are self directed; that is, they are not offered as proof to the teacher that the student has read the book. They involve readers in sharing with other readers books they have enjoyed. A book talk briefly introduces the audience to the plot, main characters, and the problem that the characters encounter in the story (Hudson, 2016). It is no more than two minutes long.

---

### Sample Book Talk for *I Am Henry Finch* by Alexis Deacon

We are all unique. We have our individual thoughts. I've read a story that shows us this through a heroic red bird, Henry Finch. He puts his stamp on this book with his own red fingerprint. Find out how he becomes a hero and saves his flock by the power of thinking. **Read *I Am Henry Finch*** — you won't be sorry!

— Amber, Grade 4 student

---

*Authors Share (or Author's Chair):* Used during Writers Workshop, authors' sharing time allows students to present works-in-progress or works that have been published, in order to receive audience feedback and engage in group problem-solving. Work can be at any stage of the writing process, including oral rehearsal. Ten to 15 minutes is recommended. Some classrooms designate a chair for the author to sit in while sharing work. Michelle changed the name to Authors Share in her classroom to emphasize that the process can be used to get feedback at any stage of the writing process. Her students had thought that Author's Chair was meant for presenting finished pieces of writing only.

Michelle reports that ever since she began to routinely include Authors Share, she has observed a marked improvement in students' motivation to write interesting pieces. As with student-led book talks, it is the opinions of their peers that matter most to students.

## Close Connections: Talking and Drawing

The processes of talking, drawing, reading, and writing are closely connected socially, emotionally, and cognitively. They are even neurologically connected, using the same part of the human brain. It makes sense to include them together in classroom literacy activities. Here are Terry's pertinent notes based on a 2016 conference presentation by Brian Cambourne at the 3rd Baltic Sea — 17th Nordic Literacy Conference in Turku, Finland:

> Literacy activities require meaning-making processes. Progress in literacy is a continuous process of knowledge building. Oral language and written language are part of a continuous spectrum, the way art, drawing, and music are. For educators, the pedagogical implications involve a different kind of teaching, where opportunities are created for the construction of meaning making. The type of classroom based on a meaning-making discourse would reflect continual cycles, with continual demonstration and modelling, with recurring opportunities for learners to be involved in "rich tasks" of reading, writing, talking, drawing, and so on. The process of becoming literate — according to this discourse — involves cycles of constructing and re-constructing.

As stated in the introduction to this book, we conceptualize literacy as embracing reading, writing, and oral communication along with digital technologies and multimodal texts, where written modes are combined with oral, visual, audio, gestural, tactile, and spatial patterns of meaning. This means that the many and varied processes of meaning making Cambourne refers to are at the heart of the kind of vibrant classroom we advocate in this book. These classrooms are

> characterized by students who engage in continual cycles of talking, listening, reading, writing, drawing, acting, creating 3D models, and other meaning-making behaviors. The continuous sharing and discussion of the content and structure of the final products of these rich tasks means that learners are continually de-constructing and re-constructing their own and each other's knowledge . . . [T]he continuous cycles of sharing and discussing . . . provide multiple opportunities for explicitly "naming" and describing the meaning-making processes they're engaged in. This means they are constantly developing their metacognitive awareness of how learning, thinking, and knowledge build "work." (Cambourne, 2017, p. 23)

As Michelle put it so succinctly, "This is *meaning-making*. Every day."

# 4

## Playing with Language Out Loud

BL DoC

*Language creativity, or the artful use of language, is central to children's emotional, cognitive, and social development and education, as well as to communication in general.*

— Teresa Cremin and Janet Maybin, 2013, p. 276

*It just sounds more special when you use poetry. Things become not ordinary anymore — like magic.*

— Sadi, Grade 4 student

Creativity is central in the playful use of language found in forms such as poetry, rhymes, and songs.

Cremin and Maybin (2013, p. 285) explain, "Creativity in and through language is not only evident right from the beginning of life, but is also clearly important for aesthetic, developmental, educational, and wider social functions." In their article on creativity in and through language, they write, for example, "It appears that children's creativity *in* language through rhyme, rhythm, imagery, and play with meaning is a driving force that continues across the lifespan, from nonsense words, riddles, jokes, made up languages and scatological playground rhymes through verbal insult dueling and hip-hop raps." They say, as well, "Children's creativity *through* language to construct identity and relationship, and to generate alternative realities allowing innovative thinking and experimentation, also appears to be *crucial for their emotional and social development, and for intellectual innovation*" (p. 285, emphasis added).

Beyond the creativity that children can exercise, teachers have opportunities to demonstrate creativity through language:

> Modeling the imaginative use of spoken language, through oral storytelling, discussion, teacher in role work, or in the context of improvised poetry performance, for example, also involves taking risks, tolerating uncertainty, and the adoption of a playful, improvisational, and arguably artistic stance. (Cremin & Maybin, 2013, p. 283)

Further, within the context of playful language use, there are prime opportunities to enrich vocabulary. Teaching words in context, teaching definitions, allowing opportunities for deep processing, promoting active engagement that goes beyond definitional knowledge, and providing multiple exposures to words that will prove useful to the learner in many contexts, all enhance vocabulary acquisition (Beck, McKeown, & Kucan, 2002; Stahl, 2005).

## Let's Begin with Poetry

The use of chants, poems, raps, and rhymes can be engaging to students at all grade levels, from Kindergarten to Grade 8. Collections by Jack Prelutsky and poems by Loris Lesynksi and Sheree Fitch, for example, are especially recommended.

For Michelle's class, we have modelled the rhythm, rhyme, and fun of saying a rap-like poem out loud by using Loris Lesynski's "Boogie" poem. The poem was projected on the Smart Board, and as the teachers, we loudly chanted:

> A boogie is a dance
> and a boogie is a jive
> and a boogie's just another way of saying I'm alive.
> Boogie in an elevator.
> Boogie in the street.
> Anything's a boogie if it has a buh-buh-beat . . .

The students kept the beat with their hands and feet.

On the second reading, the students were invited to join in, for choral reading, while continuing to keep the beat.

They enjoyed playing with the poem:

- "I liked the Boogie rap 'cause it was super funny. I liked keeping the beat with our hands and feet." (Scott)
- "I like the way the teachers did it. They were singing it really good — they were really good rappers. It was fun 'cause we got to keep the beat, and then we all did it together, and at the end we slowed it down when it faded out. It was fun!" (Mikko)

After ongoing weekly, if not daily, exposure to published poems and choral reading of them, students will be ready to create their own poetry. A sample activity from Michelle's Grade 3–4 class follows.

## Creating Multimodal Poetry

The multimodal poems created in this activity combine oral and written poetry with visual images and animated digital productions using Keynote. The activity involves matching visual images and poetic language. It illustrates two things: (1) that listening to poetic language and viewing related visual images can stimulate discussion, collaboration, and the creation of original multimodal poetry, and (2) that providing evocative visual images, the opportunity to collaborate, and some simple, open-ended sentence starters creates a workshop atmosphere where everyone becomes engaged in creating multimodal poetry.

The whole Loris Lesynski poem appears as the illustrated book *Dirty Dog Boogie*.

Before the students in Michelle's class began the poetry activity, they had listened to and viewed *The Crow's Tale* and discussed how the rhyming verse and beautiful illustrations enhanced the story (see Chapter 3). They had also gained prior knowledge of poetic features of rhyme, rhythm, beat, and repetition through activities investigating song lyrics and poetry anthologies. The teachers had modelled an oral poetry reading, Loris Lesynski's *Dirty Dog Boogie*.

## Overview of the Activity

### Materials You Will Need

- A well-illustrated read-aloud text written in poetic form
- Many evocative, colorful images from books, calendars, real paintings, and photos — at least twice as many as the number of students in the class
- iPads or other devices for publishing

### Steps

*Students have the option of working collaboratively in pairs or trios or on their own.*

1. Students listen to and look at a read-aloud text, listening for rhyme, rhythm, and musical language and paying attention to how visual images are connected to the text.
2. Students collaborate on choosing an illustration; they discuss it and explore poetic language to match.
3. Students orally compose and then write an original poem.
4. Students publish multimodal poetry using the images they have chosen and the poems they have written.
5. Students share and discuss each other's poems using Author's Chair (which, in Michelle's class, is called "Authors Share").

### Accommodations

- If needed to help some students get under way, provide a sentence starter, for example, "Imagine . . .," or "I feel . . .," on the Smart Board or chalkboard.
- Arrange for an educational assistant or trained volunteer to scribe the written lines of poetry for students, as needed. The students can say their poems orally and have the lines written for them.

### Assessment

To help develop a basis for assessment, circulate and listen to student talk; beyond that, ask students to share their compositions during and after writing.

Assess use of poetic language in dialogue with students: discuss rhyming, if used; the rhythm of the lines; and how the pictures and words relate to one another.

During whole-group sharing, assess finished products for poetic language and its relationship to the visual image; consider, too, how any animation used enhances the multimodal poem.

## Day 1: The Read-Aloud and Collaborative Poetry Creation

This lesson is founded on a read-aloud of *Buttercup's Lovely Day* by Carolyn Beck, but any picture book written in poetry would be appropriate. *Buttercup's Lovely Day* happens to be in rhyming poetry, but Michelle's students were also familiar with the free verse of Carl Sandburg's "Fog," for example, and had discussed the idea that not all poems rhyme. They had listened to and read *Imagine a Day* and *Imagine a Night*, and were influenced by Sarah Thomson's non-rhyming poems that accompany the illustrations.

BEFORE: Introduce the story. As with *The Crow's Tale*, Buttercup the calf tells about her day in rhyming poetry. Ask the students to listen to how it sounds, how Buttercup's words match her day, and how musical the calf's language is. Some words she even makes up. Direct the students to listen for those.

DURING: We read the book in tandem, allowing time for students to examine the illustrations.

AFTER THE READ-ALOUD: We began by asking each other what we had liked about the book . . .

TERRY: I liked the way Buttercup could tell us all about her ordinary day using beautiful poetry.

MICHELLE: I like the kind of day she had. I could have pictured everything without looking at the illustrations. I also thought how nice and pleasant it would be to be a cow.

*There was laughter among the students.*

ONE BOY: Yeah, you would have no responsibilities!

MICHELLE: Yes, you still would. You would have to go along with the other cows and do things the way cows do.

After that, we asked the students what they had liked, receiving responses like these:

- "I liked the illustrations. They matched the words."
- "I liked the way it went from morning to night . . ."
- "I liked that the cow did the talking and everything rhymed."

We also asked the students if they had noticed any made-up words. We returned to the text to find them, discovering, for example, the *fluzz* of the flies, a drift of *murk*, the mossy *musk*, and *a bloop*, a swoop.

Having provided the students with an exemplar, Michelle formally introduced the activity to them with these instructions:

"You are going to choose some pictures and create poems to match the way Buttercup did. You can also write short poems like the ones in *Imagine a Day*, the book we read last month, and we also have *Imagine a Night*, as well as some paintings from a calendar. You can work with a partner, choose your picture, and talk about how to make a poem using the picture to inspire you. You can compose your poems out loud and then write them down when you are ready. We will share our poems using Authors Share and then publish the poems with the matching illustrations tomorrow, using our iPads."

Pictures and pages from books, as well as whole books, were spread on the centre carpet so that students could move around and choose images that appealed to them. Some students found partners or, in one case, formed a trio based on their attraction to a particular image. They talked about it and then agreed they could work on a poem together based on that picture. They took the image to a table where they continued to examine and discuss it. They explored language and words to contribute to a poem, orally composing first and then requesting paper to record it.

One pair of girls, sitting side by side, propped up their picture in front of them and stared at it for some time before discussing it and jointly considering possible lines of poetry.

A: Imagine being there . . .
B: Yes, if you were a . . .
A: You could . . .
B: Yes, and . . .
A: It would feel . . .

Their poem was based on a picture of children riding bicycles above trees. To get it, they talked, tried out lines, and then wrote:

*We are there*
*Bike riding down*
*The long beautiful road*
*Up we go*
*Into the trees*
*With a nice autumn glow.*

A trio of boys chose to look at a painting of a local (North Bay) scene, Duchesnay Falls, with a person leaning against a tree looking out at the river. Here's an excerpt from their talk:

JAY: I would like to sit on the trunk of that huge tree!
LARRY: Me too! I've been to that falls. Have you?
JAY: Yeah, but I don't remember that tree. *Laughter*
PATRICK: If you sat there, you could just stare, just watch the water.
LARRY: It looks like there's a wind . . .
PATRICK: Just a breeze, though. Look. The leaves and the guy's hair aren't moving that much.
JAY: Let's say, "Imagine sitting on the trunk of a big old tree . . .,"
PATRICK: Yeah, then, "Watching the water flowing."
LARRY: And feel the wind? I mean, the breeze? Let's say, "Feeling the breeze blowing!"
ALL: YES!

They then wrote:

*Imagine sitting on the trunk of a big old tree*
*Watching the water flowing,*
*Feeling the breeze blowing . . .*

Their talk continued.

LARRY: Should we add more?
JAY: Let's read it again.
*One reads it aloud.*
PATRICK: No. No, it's good.
JAY: Yeah, yeah, it's a poem.
LARRY: Yes, it's *our* poem!

## Day 2: Publishing Multimodal Poetry

Students transcribed their poems from day 1 by taking photos of their featured pictures by iPad and by using the powerful presentation app Keynote.

Talia based her poem on a painting from *Imagine a Day* by Sara L. Thomson. Rob Gonsalves's painting shows children climbing up the reflection of a tree in a lake. Talia published this poem, using animated text:

*Imagine a day*
*Where you can climb and climb*
*Going up water reflections*

*Time after time*
*The water soars through your feet*
*And the reflection holds you up*
*Through stormy days,*
*Hard times*
*And the coldest nights.*

Based on a calendar painting of a tiger and a tortoise looking at each other, Ali published this poem, called "Happy Tiger":

*I am a tiger*
*As happy as can be*
*Mostly because a turtle*
*[Is] looking at me.*
*Out in the pired [sic] lands*
*As open as air*
*The wind is blowing through my orange hair.*
*Now I am sleepy*
*Under this tree.*
*A small nap would not hurt, you see.*

And two boys, Jake and Graham, collaborated to create a poem based on a painting of a narwhal swimming underwater in the Arctic:

*Under the ice*
*I swim along*
*Until the day is gone*
*All my friends go home*
*And I sleep under the stones.*

*Reflection:* The students found using iPads to photograph their scenes and then importing the photos into Keynote on the class iPads easy. Once they had done this, they typed in their poems. They particularly enjoyed experimenting with the app's text animation features in order to emphasize key words. They discussed their choices with peers at their tables before finalizing their presentations.

The students showed their poetry presentations during a celebratory classroom Authors Share. After each author or authors presented, students gave positive comments.

The first four lines of the multimodal poem "Happy Tiger" appear with images here.

# Using Texts to Spark Thought and Talk about Words

In some texts, the words themselves call out for attention. Noticing the different features of words, such as how they sound, how they look, and how they are used in a text, is interesting in its own right, but thinking and talking about words can also improve metacognitive awareness about words. This, in turn, elevates and broadens the way students use words in speech and in writing. The model texts mentioned below provide insights into the uses and value of words.

The books are best introduced through read-alouds, followed by discussions about how words are used in each particular text. They can then be left on display for students to examine.

## Collecting and Categorizing Words

The illustrated text, *Max's Words*, demonstrates how one can literally play with words. In the book by Kate Banks, illustrated by Boris Kulikov, Max's brothers have conventional collections of stamps and coins. Max decides to collect words. He collects them under interesting categories, such as words that were said to him, for example, "Go away." He and his brothers come to realize that unlike stamps or coins, the order of the words makes a huge difference. They soon collaborate to create stories using the words.

### Possible Activities After the Read-Aloud

Familiarity with a picture book like this can lead to a variety of activities. To facilitate these, cut out a big collection of words from magazines or discarded books (enough for a dozen for each pair of students).

- In partners, students can create collages. They can compare the different fonts and colors and discuss their impact. They can also go back to the text and talk about how the illustrator uses fonts for effect (Kindergarten to Grade 3).
- Another activity is for students to choose four or five words from the book to illustrate and explain orally. Possible words include *ragged*, *scrambled*, *rapidly*, *ordered*, and *darted*. This activity works well in Grades 1 and 2.
- Invite students in Grade 2 or 3 to talk in pairs about possible word categories using the cut-out words supplied. They can organize the words and tell the class why they have been so categorized. Typical categories include feeling words, action words, and words about food (taken from grocery ads, for example). Students can compare their categories to Max's categories.
- From a bank of cut-out words, students can create a story (Kindergarten to Grade 4).

## Gaining the Gift of Words

Like *Max's Words*, *My Two Blankets* by Irena Kobald works well with Kindergarten to Grade 4 students. The book is beautifully illustrated by Freya Blackwood. It is especially appropriate where there are English language learners in the classroom. In this story, a girl named Cartwheel moves to a new country to be safe from war but finds everything strange.

> Nobody spoke like I did.
> When I went out, it was like standing

Under a waterfall of strange sounds . . .
*I felt like I wasn't me anymore.*

At night Cartwheel takes solace under her old blanket, which features symbols and animals from the girl's former home.

Then Cartwheel makes a friend in the park, and the new girl brings her the gift of words. As she tries out the unfamiliar words under her old blanket, they start to sound "warm and soft" and she begins to weave a new blanket. In the end, she has a friend, two blankets, and the realization that "I will always be me."

*Possible Activities After the Read-Aloud*

- Hold a grand conversation focused on these questions: How do words and pictures connect in this text? How do you learn new words?
- Engage the students in visual art based on the picture book. Using textiles, paints, or pencil crayons, they can illustrate two blankets, using associated words and symbols. Arrange to display their art and do a class gallery walk in pairs to discuss the artwork. Ask: "How do the pictures and words connect?"
- Provide students with cards or posted lists with descriptive words (adjectives or adverbs). Invite students to choose words that describe them and to draw self-portraits using words that relate to them personally. Allow them to share orally with a partner or in a small group.

## Exploring Action Words and Character Traits

*The Most Magnificent Thing* is explored further in Chapter 5.

For making a stapleless book, see instructions on the ReadWriteThink website, #48 of Classroom Resources, Student Interactive.

In *The Most Magnificent Thing* by Ashley Spires, a tenacious girl struggles and succeeds in building her most magnificent thing. The picture book is notable for its rich vocabulary, especially verbs. It is well worth exploring, especially with students in Grades 3 to 6.

- Invite students to use passages from the text to create illustrated, stapleless books of verbs. Be sure to share story excerpts that highlight verbs, for example: she *tinkers and hammers and measures* and *smoothes and wrenches and fiddles*. The girl persists. She also *saws, glues, adjusts, twists, tweaks, fastens*, and more. Her efforts reach a crisis point when she *smashes, jams,* and *pummels.*
- *The Most Magnificent Thing* also lends itself to a discussion of character traits. With the whole class, discuss character traits and related synonyms, for example, tenacity, determination, persistence, perseverance, diligence, grit, and doggedness. In pairs, students can discuss times when they had to be persistent to complete something.

## Confusion by Homonym

In the context of a Grade 5 classroom where there is a special day to celebrate vocabulary, we can infer the hilarious results from the title: *Miss Alaineus: A Vocabulary Disaster*. Students, especially those in Grades 5 to 8, enjoy this book by Debra Frasier.

For a whole-group activity, provide multisyllabic words orally. Discuss what they mean, and challenge students to separate the words that sound similar, but mean something quite different (homonyms). For example, *mystery* could be heard as "Miss Story" or "Mister E"; *forebears* could be interpreted as "four bears." Provide initial examples. Discuss tips on how to find words that can be mistaken in this way. (Hint: The first syllable has a homonym, or word of the same spelling or sound, but different meaning.)

## Playing with Words to Augment Vocabulary

Learning new vocabulary requires more than learning the definition or even learning the word in context. An example can go much further to make a new word come alive and "stick." For instance, if you wanted to teach the word *iridescent*, you could make the connection to a previously enjoyed story, *The Crow's Tale*. You could show the illustration of the crow's feathered wing as it was towards the end of the book, and discuss how the colors demonstrate *iridescence*.

Teachers can go far beyond providing definitions and contexts by giving students opportunities to use new words in meaningful ways. Students who are both learning new words and learning how to learn vocabulary need engaging methods that provide experiential learning to help them construct meanings in ways relevant to them (Nagy, 1988).

The activities that follow provide such opportunities.

### Use Play Contexts

For early primary students (Junior Kindergarten to Grade 1), Shelley Stagg Peterson suggests making use of play contexts (activity centres) to support vocabulary development. She notes, "Teachers can support vocabulary development by participating in children's play using new vocabulary appropriate to the play context." She provides this example:

> Introduce words through reading and rereading a story or poem, inviting children to explore meanings of words they encounter. Create further play settings in which children can apply the new vocabulary in their interactions with peers and objects. When reading Jan Thornhill's *Over in the Meadow* (Maple Tree Press, 2004), for example, teachers might say, "I wonder what the muskrat was doing when she burrowed in the reeds. Pretend you're the mother muskrat. What do you use to burrow? Why do you want to burrow in the reeds? What else might you burrow into?" After discussing other animals that burrow (perhaps while showing pictures of frogs, chipmunks, clams, moles, cicadas, snakes, burrowing owls, and other burrowing creatures), along with reasons for burrowing, children might create and play with playdough figures of burrowers. (Peterson, 2016, pp. 2–3)

### Teach Vocabulary Explicitly

Try using the following steps suggested by Beck, McKeown, and Kucan (2002) to teach vocabulary explicitly during whole-class lessons and discussions; you can also extend the instruction by adding drama.

1. Show the word and have the students say the word, clap the word, and repeat the word in different ways, in various voices. For example, they might whisper the word, say it slowly, and sing the word.

2. To clarify any misconceptions, ask the students for the word's meaning. Students can discuss with a partner how to show the meaning. For example, for the word *fragrant*, someone might mime picking a flower and smelling it, smiling.
3. Have individual students orally use the word in a sentence, and if the word lends itself, they can act it out. For the word *exhausted*, they might say, "When we got home, we were *exhausted*," place hands on foreheads, flop forward as though to fall, and walk very slowly.

After the last step, the words can be added to the word wall.

Word walls are classroom displays of words printed on cards, arranged so that students can see them readily, especially when they are writing. Typically arranged alphabetically, they can be lists based on any category relevant to the students at a particular time. For example, they may be lists of high-frequency words the students are working on to build writing fluency, lists of words relating to a current science study, or technical words they are learning during units on geometry or specific visual arts, such as sculpture.

**Walking the Wall**

Keep the word wall active and interactive by providing time for students to "walk the wall," to walk along in pairs to discuss and add sticky notes with rhyming words, synonyms, antonyms, and so on.

## Provide Repeated Exposure to Words

Research also shows that repetition and multiple exposures to vocabulary items, where students encounter words repeatedly in a variety of contexts, is vital for learning new words (Stahl, 2005). Classroom activities that allow repeated exposure to words include shared reading, choral reading, and storytelling (Chapter 7), Readers theatre (Chapter 8), and use of interactive word walls.

## Let Students Illustrate New Words

Because children's drawings communicate thought (Eisner, 2002), an effective evidence-based strategy is to have the students choose four new words to illustrate. Having groups of students illustrate words on index cards or in writing journals also provides an opportunity for vocabulary review (LaBrocca & Morrow, 2016, p. 155). In Michelle's classroom, the students stated that they enjoyed this activity.

Michelle has used stapleless books for her students to record and illustrate "funny words" inspired by *Hooray for Diffendoofer Day!* by Jack Prelutsky and Dr. Seuss. Students brainstormed possible words in small groups and chose seven words (stapleless books have eight pages, including the title page). Their chosen words included *jiggledy*, *dodo bird*, *goofus*, and *mooshy*.

## Turn Word Activities into Games

Beck and her colleagues (2002) provide examples of many great activities that can be turned into games, including Applause, Applause; Word Associations; and Idea Completion.

- *Applause, Applause* is a fun game in which students indicate, by level of applause, how much (a lot, a little, not at all) they would like to be described by certain words. Their clapping, for example, might reveal whether they would like to be described as joyous, menacing, hopeful, greedy, mature, or enthusiastic.

- In *Word Associations*, students (working individually, in pairs, or in small groups) are asked to pair a new word with another word or phrase and explain why the pairing works. For the words *catastrophe*, *fragrant*, and *fragile*, teams might be asked:

    Which word goes with perfume? (*fragrant*)
    Which word goes with fire in Fort McMurray? (*catastrophe*)
    Which word goes with glass vase? (*fragile*)

- *Idea Completion* games require students to use their own words to explain the meanings of new words as they complete sentence stems such as these:

    The crow's feathers looked *iridescent* because . . .
    The team was *victorious* when . . .
    The driver was *distracted* by . . .

## Explore Puns and Idioms

Understanding puns and idioms is a subtle, but deep aspect of really knowing and appreciating the cultural richness of one's own language or another language. Further, these language structures can be fun to explore. Books that feature wordplay and idioms include *Why the Banana Split* by Rick Walton (Grades 1 to 3) and for junior grades, Debra Frasier's *Miss Alaineus: A Vocabulary Disaster* (see www.debrafrasier.com). A good source for puns is www.punoftheday.com. Here are some sample puns on which to base oral discussion, illustration, and analysis:

    I wondered why the baseball was getting bigger. Then it hit me.
    I was going to get a brain transplant, but then I changed my mind.
    Yesterday I accidentally swallowed some food coloring. The doctor said
        I'm okay, but I feel I've dyed a little inside.
    The elevator is a great invention. On so many levels.

English language learners find idioms especially challenging. What might they make of the idiom *fly by the seat of your pants*, for example? Mystified learners, as well as some other students, may require explicit explanation of the meanings.

Exploring common idioms through classroom talk, art, and drama is a fun and memorable way of becoming acquainted with a challenging feature of the English language. Students can explore an idiom by talking first in small groups about what it might mean, then discussing their guesses in the large group, where the teacher can clarify and provide examples. Drawing cartoons of the literal meaning of an idiom can result in funny variations. For example, *you are driving me up the wall* could be shown by a car going up the side of a brick wall. Other idioms that lend themselves to being illustrated include *it's raining cats and dogs*; *my head is in the clouds*; and *what he said went in one ear and out the other*. Idioms can also be listed and then acted out in small groups with the rest of the class guessing which idiom a group is presenting (*in one ear and out the other* works well here).

---

### More on How to Play with Language

Playing with language orally and thereby fostering word awareness is enjoyable and stimulating for students at any grade level. Here are some final suggestions organized by grade range.

---

*Kindergarten to Grade 2*

- Create rhyming words and nonsense rhymes orally (e.g., *cat, wat, zat*) to bolster phonemic awareness.
- Create a fun and funny class-illustrated alphabet book modelled on *Dr. Seuss's ABCs*.
- Replace words in well-known nursery rhymes by inserting a different first consonant. For example, "Mary had a little lamb" could become "Wary wad a wittle wamb."
- Read lots of poems aloud. *Read Aloud Poems for the Very Young*, selected by Jack Prelutsky, is one good anthology.
- Listen to songs with clear words that are easy to sing along with. For example, songs by Raffi are very engaging for this age group.

*Grades 3 to 6*

- Investigate poetry out loud. Use whole-class choral reading to enjoy the sounds of rhythmic, rhyming words. Poetry books by Sheree Fitch, Jack Prelutsky, Loris Lesysnki, and more are rich sources of poems meant to be read aloud.
- For a great beginning-of-the-school-year activity, have students create alliterative sentences with their names. Model first.
    Marvelous Michelle makes magical meatballs.
    Terrible Terry tells terrifically tall tales.
- Let students listen to songs and raps appealing to this age group; for example, they might like will.i.am's affirmative raps, such as "Hall of Fame" (suitable for Grades 5 to 8, as well).

*Grades 5 to 8*

- Explore the worlds of puns, jokes, and idioms. They are part of our oral language culture. Investigate how they work.
- Use song lyrics and raps to explore poetic expression.
- Investigate poetry where serious topics are treated with humor. Sheree Fitch's *If You Could Wear My Sneakers: A Book About Children's Rights* and Jon Scieszka's *Math Curse* and *Science Verse* are three recommended titles.
- Investigate the rich poetic and linguistic features of (appropriate) pop songs and raps: beat, rhythm, rhyme, repetition, and alliteration can make the songs, poems, and raps fun to sing or chant orally. Students can then create their own raps.

Finally, keep in mind the *power* of the word. Vygotsky said that "the sense" of a word is the sum of all the psychological events aroused in consciousness by that word. He also described *sense* metaphorically as the "storm cloud of thought that produces the shower of words" (see Smagorinsky, 2001, p. 145). Although we can have fun with them, words are more than playthings. They have power. They can be used to build knowledge, identity, and community.

# 5

## Optimizing the Impact of Read-Alouds

*BL Doc.*

*Recognize the importance of reading aloud to children. Let children hear text structures that expose them to language beyond their own control. Reading aloud to children of any age will sketch for them a landscape of features into which their own language usage may expand.*

— Marie Clay, 2004, p. 10

*BL Doc.*

*A story read out loud can take you on a reading ride. Going up and then back down. Or it could have a flip. You never quite know what's coming next.*

— Dana, Grade 3 student

If we want our students to engage in *meaningful* talk, they need something significant to talk about. A well-illustrated picture book with a perplexing, humorous, or shocking problem, memorable characters, and a vividly portrayed setting can provide that *something* that stimulates them to respond on a personal level. Given the opportunity to talk about a thought-provoking text, students can delve into problems, questions, and feelings raised by the story text and images, and become motivated to discuss issues more deeply and critically than they might normally do. Furthermore, if students are presented with these texts through teacher read-alouds, they may be able to enjoy texts beyond their present levels of reading ability and oral language capability. Marie Clay points out that when we read aloud to our students, we can "sketch for them a landscape." And as one of Michelle's students put it, we can take them on a "reading ride." We can then talk about it.

### Take Students on a Reading Ride

In this chapter, we explore how to optimize the potential of daily read-aloud time. Teachers can do so by selecting high-quality literature and by providing opportunities for students to discuss these texts with the goal of collaboratively constructing deep meanings and engaging in literacy thinking and learning at higher levels. Therefore, the benefits of read-alouds go beyond the goal of getting students to talk, although that goal is worthy. We are also providing students with language models that can extend and expand their oral language use.

For more on this topic, you may want to check out *Good Books Matter* by Shelley Stagg Peterson and Larry Swartz.

---

### Five Criteria for Selecting High-Quality Children's Books

These criteria apply to both fictional and informational texts.
1. Appealing to children, both visually and conceptually
2. Good dramatic story and/or fascinating facts
3. Fantastic or real-life stories told in original ways
4. Not too explicitly moralistic (A moral message embedded subtly or humorously is better received.)
5. Relevant to learners: accurate, factual, well researched

---

According to research studies, higher levels of literacy learning share two common elements. First, the form of the discourse is *interactive discussion*. This form allows open, freely unfolding student talk, not bound by the traditional, teacher-dominated *recitation* pattern (discussed in Chapter 2). Second, the focus of the discussion is on personal meaning-making, thus going beyond literal-level comprehension.

Going beyond literal-level comprehension means engaging in meaning making at more complex levels. Rather than simply retelling the main events of a story, for example, a deeper discussion may involve examining how the author and illustrator organized the events and messages in the story to achieve a certain impact on the reader and viewer. Instead of requiring the reader to recall the names of the characters, meaning making at the higher levels may involve delving into the characters' motivations. As Hoffman (2011) puts it, "Children are entirely capable of engaging in higher level literacy practices when their meaning making is facilitated by teacher supports and interactive discussion" (p. 184).

This chapter presents ideas and strategies for tapping into the full potential of daily read-alouds. We begin with how to choose texts that can stimulate dynamic, interactive *real discussions*. This is followed by suggested strategies for infusing classroom read-alouds with opportunities for interactive discussions characterized by higher-level critical thinking.

We have chosen to focus on illustrated fiction texts for this chapter because of their diversity and availability; however, the strategies discussed apply to many nonfiction and media texts, as well.

We have identified three selection categories for texts that provide students with something worth listening to and talking about.

- **Provocative and controversial texts** are worth considering. What makes a text provocative? By *provocative*, we mean texts that provoke a personal response — positive or negative. The response can take the form of voicing one's opinion in a discussion, in writing, or in drawing about one's thoughts and feelings as in Sketch to Stretch *Plus* (see Chapter 3), or engaging in further reading on the topic or about the author or illustrator. What makes a text controversial? By *controversial*, we mean texts that may have been challenged, sometimes by parents or school authorities. Controversial texts that have been publicly identified as challenged invite critical thinking responses through talk, writing, and more reading, particularly by students in Grades 4 and up.

Note that sometimes the controversy takes place right in the classroom among the students. For example, after listening to a read-aloud of Leo Lionni's *Frederick*, about a dreamy mouse in a family of mice busily getting ready for winter, some Grade 1 students in Terry's class objected to Frederick's apparent lack of work ethic: "It's not fair! The other mice are doing all the work, and Frederick is just sitting there!" There were others, though, who defended his artistic contributions: "Frederick gave them words, colors, and poetry when they needed them!"

After telling the story of "Goldilocks and the Three Bears" to his Junior Kindergarten class, Dave Shields reported that four-year-old Hannah was outraged by the behavior of Goldilocks: "She should not go into someone's house and eat their food and break their things!" For Hannah, the story of Goldilocks was provocative. The rest of the students offered different opinions, saying maybe Goldilocks was tired and hungry, and didn't mean to break anything.

*This is the beauty and the power of* talk. *As with all controversy and disagreement, we can use talk to* voice, listen to, *and* consider our differences in opinion.

---

## Why Use Potentially Controversial Texts in the Classroom?

High-quality literature, including controversial texts, has the potential to stimulate students to

- *talk critically* about the texts and any controversies pertaining to them
- *address issues* rather than avoid or ignore them (Although many students may struggle to cope with teasing and bullying, talking about a fictional story in the safety of the classroom with a teacher's guidance can provide a safe venue for expressing diverse thoughts and feelings, and learning how to listen and accept differences.)
- *write feelingly* about their own responses to strong texts or produce their own texts that have an impact similar to the texts they have been exposed to
- *read more extensively* about the topics considered controversial and about the authors and illustrators

---

- **Problem-based texts** present a question or dilemma for their readers or listeners to ponder, and may present one solution among other possibilities, sparking lively follow-up discussions. For example, *The Red Lemon* presents the problem with its title and with the cover illustration. A farmer holds a basket of yellow lemons in one hand, while looking in shock at a single red lemon in his other hand. *What to do?* Problem-based texts include, as a subset, texts that present moral or social justice issues, such as *I Want My Hat Back* by Jon Klassen (Primary) and *Four Feet, Two Sandals* by Karen Lynn Williams and Khadra Mohammed (Junior).
- **Evocative texts** are characterized by striking visuals that suggest or evoke a story or atmosphere. Examples include Chris Van Allsburg's *The Mysteries of Harris Burdick* and *Imagine a Day* and *Imagine a Night*, both by Sarah L. Thomson, illustrated by Rob Gonsalves. This category also includes some wordless books, such as *Journey* by Aaron Becker and *Tuesday* by David Wiesner.

# Provocative Texts and Talking About Them

One particularly provocative picture book will be investigated here. *17 Things I'm Not Allowed to Do Anymore* by Jenny Offill is suitable for students in Grades 1 to 6. The text is noteworthy for its marvelous illustrations and exceptional writing which are juxtaposed in sometimes contradictory ways to create laugh-out-loud scenes. A few other texts that can be seen as provocative or controversial are then discussed.

## Talk About Ideas: Before, During, and After the Read-Aloud

Jenny Offill's humorous book is narrated by a curious, disruptive girl in Grade 2 who pushes the limits of what is acceptable in school and at home.

The illustrations by Nancy Carpenter combine cartoon-style drawings and photo collage, with some of the real objects the young girl uses when getting into trouble inserted. For example, when she has the idea to staple her brother's hair to the pillow, a photo of a stapler is included. The episodic story is augmented by the clever illustrations, which tell us more about the events and invite inferential thinking. Each incident is worth a full conversation by itself.

Each event begins with "I had an idea . . ." and (except for the last) ends with "I am not allowed to . . . anymore." For example, "I had an idea to order a different dinner from my mother." "I am not allowed to pretend my mother is a waitress anymore." The girl has a series of clashes with her teacher, her brother, and her mother and several times gets into trouble for her interest in beavers.

To organize this read-aloud and support student thinking and discussion, use a *before-during-after* structure.

### Before the Read-Aloud

Present objects such as a stapler and a bottle of glue to groups of four, and ask them to discuss ideas on how these items can be used. What might be some good ideas? What would not be good ideas for their use? Here's what two of Michelle's students said:

- "A good idea for glue is using it for crafts, to glue paper together.
    A not good idea is to put glue on a chair so someone sticks to it." (Jack, Grade 3)
- "A good idea for a stapler is to staple paper to make your own book.
    A not good idea is to staple the pages of a good book together so someone couldn't read it." (Larry, Grade 4)

Provide other small groups with pictures of animals that typically live in the wild, for example, a beaver, a deer, or an eagle. Have them discuss whether it would be a good idea to have any of these animals as pets. Allow each group time to present their ideas to the large group.

Introduce the book cover and title, and invite students to speculate about some of the things the girl on the cover might not be allowed to do anymore, and why. We also asked the class to consider what kind of character this girl might be.

- "She looks curious." (Ali, Grade 3)
- "And mischievous." (Sadi, Grade 4)
- "And kind of funny, too!" (Torry, Grade 4)

*17 Things I'm Not Allowed to Do Anymore*

"During my placement in a Grade 6 class, I used this book when teaching *inference*. I asked my students what they could infer from the title and the cover illustrations as well as what they could infer about the child's relationship with her mother or teacher. We also compared the illustrations and the girl's words in several episodes, in order to infer what else was happening at the time. For example, the girl says, 'I had an idea to give my brother the gift of cauliflower.' The illustration shows the girl using her fork to catapult the cauliflower across the table to her brother. She then says, 'I am not allowed to give the gift of cauliflower anymore.'"
— Brendan Callas, B.Ed. student

**The Strategy: Combined read-aloud and shared reading with talk before, during, and after**

*During the Read-Aloud*

Read the story aloud and together with the students, in shared reading style, say the repeated words, "I am not allowed to . . . anymore."

Stop two or three times to examine the illustrations and infer what else is going on besides what the narrator supplies. For example, when the girl is claiming to "give the gift of cauliflower," discuss what else the students know based on what they can glean from the illustration.

In Michelle's class, the students needed time to laugh. Not surprisingly, they laughed loudest and longest where the girl has the idea to show Joey Whipple her underpants. The cartoon-style drawing shows her doing a cartwheel. "I am not allowed to show Joey Whipple my underpants anymore," she intones. The students explained that underwear is always funny and that the name Joey Whipple sounded funny, too.

The students also needed time to examine the illustrations. They noticed that photos of real objects, such as a stapler, a glue bottle, a stop sign, and a U.S. dollar bill (with the girl's drawing of a beaver glued over the centre) were inserted here and there.

*After the Read-Aloud*

Ask the large group questions like these: "What do you think about the ending to this story? Do you think the main character has changed? Re-examine the final episode where the girl says, 'I'm sorry' but also says, 'I am allowed to say the opposite of what I mean forevermore.' Why do you think she is holding the stapler behind her back? Is this like other stories you have read?"

Student responses included these:

- "It means she didn't change." (Tanya, Grade 4)
- "It's like the Anansi story. He never learns his lesson either." (Patrick, Grade 4)

**Blog About Books**

Consider starting a classroom blog to share with parents and the broader community the read-alouds presented and discussed in your class. Be sure to include what the students say about the books.

Discuss how this story unfolds: is there a typical beginning, a middle, and an end? Elicit from the students the idea that the author and illustrator present a series of episodes to consider. Look back at some of them.

Pose a Big Question for students to ponder. An appropriate one is "How can you tell a good idea from a not-so-good idea?" (The text box on the next page outlines a few more titles that explore ideas.) In Michelle's classroom, this question led to discussing what to do when you have an idea that you know might be wrong. "Like stapling someone's hair to something! You don't actually do it because it might hurt, and it would get you in trouble," said Chris, a Grade 3 student.

Invite students to tell a story to their table group about a time they did something they were not supposed to. In Michelle's class, one student related the time she took apart an Oreo cookie and replaced the white filling with glue. She stopped her sister from eating it just in time, but still got in trouble for it. Have the students discuss how such events might be organized into an episodic picture book.

Return to a large-group discussion. We asked if a book like *17 Things I'm Not Allowed to Do Anymore* could make someone do something wrong. (We mentioned that some adults did not want young children to read it because they thought the book would give them the idea to do wrong things.) Lance, in Grade 4, said, grinning, "Maybe! If it was really, really funny. But not if it hurt anyone." But Aurelia, in Grade 3, said:

They wrote this book for a laugh. To make us laugh. If we went and did bad things, it wouldn't be the book's fault. It would be our own, or our parents' fault for not teaching us right and wrong. Adults shouldn't judge this book; it's for kids. I can have an idea, but I don't do it if it's wrong. This book is for fun. That's all.

For an extension, you could invite students to create collages that include drawings and pasted cut-outs of real objects from magazines. Prompt them to tell the story of their collages to their table group. Suggest that they discuss how the "real objects" enhance the story, just as they might have noticed in Nancy Carpenter's work.

---

### Having Ideas and What to Do with Them

After working with your featured provocative text, you may want to introduce a follow-up text on a related theme to help students make connections and extend the classroom discussion. Like *17 Things I'm Not Allowed to Do Anymore*, the picture books outlined below deal with ideas.

- *The Most Magnificent Thing* by Ashley Spires
  A young girl has the wonderful idea of making a most magnificent thing, but she just cannot get it right. She persists, however. She *saws and glues and adjusts*; she *stands and examines and stares*; *twists and tweaks and fastens*; and *fixes and straightens and studies*. The result is still not magnificent. She EXPLODES! "It is not her finest moment." Her assistant, shown as a dog in the illustrations, suggests a walk. She cools down and notices all her discarded pieces and how some of the wrong things are "really quite RIGHT." She gets to work . . .
  She finally succeeds in making her most magnificent thing, shown in the last illustration. The verbs used in this text provide a vivid example of how rich language can "sketch for us a landscape of features" for the extension and expansion of students' language use.
- *What Do You Do with an Idea?* by Kobi Yamada
  In this story, a little boy discovers his *idea*, pictured as a small egg-shaped creature with a crown. His idea follows him around, and he worries about what others will think of his idea. The boy soon realizes that he really likes his idea. With attention and care, the idea grows bigger . . . and the boy defends it against its critics. The boy takes ownership of his wonderful idea and helps it grow until one day it grows so big that it changes the world.
  This picture book presents higher-level, more abstract thinking about the concept of an idea and invites students to engage in a more philosophical discourse about ideas, creativity, and how they might change their worlds.

---

"This book offers many opportunities for discussions around frustrations, persistence, creativity, and appreciation. Parents will love this book because the protagonist sets such a good example for young people. Children will love this book because of the novel story and the lively illustrations."
— Whitney Underhill, B.Ed. student

You may want students to research other challenged texts on the Freedom to Read website, which lists and explains how more than 100 texts were challenged, and how the challenges were handled. See www.freedomtoread.ca

## Exploring the Controversies Around Texts

It is interesting to note that *17 Things I'm Not Allowed to Do Anymore* has been both praised and challenged by parents. The controversial book raises the question "Can a story make children do things that are wrong?" Junior-level students can debate this. They can also check out what some parents have said online.

For example, on the Goodreads site, one parent wrote: "I would never read this to my child again. It sends a very poor message . . . [I]t's a sort of satire a PARENT can enjoy, but there's no way a kid is going to get a decent message from it or understand the satire. Instead, I can only see it reinforcing bad behavior."

On the other hand, also on Goodreads, another parent wrote: "My 3 boys all enjoyed this book. They know how to tell right from wrong, so it's not like they're going to turn into juvenile delinquents or unholy terrors as a result of this book. And goodness knows, they come up with plenty of crazy ideas on their own. Books like this provide a reminder that not all impulses need to be followed up on."

Students could contrast comments like those with comments made about *The Most Magnificent Thing* by Ashley Spires. They could write a review for each book, Goodreads style.

If older students (Grades 4 to 8) explore various challenged texts, they could hold grand conversations and engage in debates to critically consider the varying opinions on the texts. Sample texts that have been challenged include *And Tango Makes Three* by Justin Richardson and Peter Parnell, illustrated by Henry Cole. At one time, in 2005, it was the number-one banned book in school libraries in the United States. It is the true story of male penguins in a New York zoo, Silo and Roy, who adopt an egg given to them by the zookeeper, hatch it (Tango), and care for it, becoming a family. The book was challenged for portraying "same-sex parents." For comparison, you could read the Canadian book, *Asha's Mums* by Rosamund Elwin and Michele Paulse. Freedom to Read reports:

> In 1997, school trustees in Surrey, B.C., banned the use of children's story books that depict same-sex parents in the elementary grades. One of the banned titles was *Asha's Mums*. A teacher, James Chamberlain, challenged the ban in court.

> In 2002, the Supreme Court of Canada declared that B.C.'s School Act required secular and non-discriminatory education. A ban on books about same-sex parents could not be legally justified.

**Prepare for Controversy**

When planning to read and discuss a controversial text, make sure you know your students, their families, and the community. Prepare your students ahead of time by discussing possible controversies, and invite students to share their own feelings and opinions, perhaps in writing first, submitted to you privately. This can be part of your pre-assessment.

Students could follow up by investigating the current status of *And Tango Makes Three*.

A provocative, potentially controversial text for students in Grades 6 to 8 is the dark and forbidding book, *The Watertower* by Gary Crew, illustrated by Steven Woolman. This multiple award–winning Australian title features striking illustrations done in acrylic paint, chalk, and pencil on black paper. The story begins ominously:

> Nobody in Preston could remember when the Watertower was built, or who had built it, but there it stood on Shooters Hill — iron legs rusted, its egg-shaped tank warped and leaking — casting a long, dark shadow across the valley, across Preston itself.

Some students might find this story disturbing. The fascinating, surrealistic illustrations suggest the presence of dark forces without really saying what they are. Two boys go into the watertower. Although one of them is reluctant, he is convinced to join in the adventure by his friend. The boy's fear is made palpable both by what the pictures say and by what is not said. *The Watertower* is worth discussing on many fronts, from dealing with peer pressure to facing fears, and for a high-level investigation of visual literacy. Because of its potential to unsettle some students, though, pre-reading preparation, knowledge of your students, and above all, *opportunities for students to talk* and respond through personal writing or drawing are advised. The book would be suitable for a small group study by mature students in Grade 8, for example.

Two other texts suitable for critical inquiry for this age group are *The Stamp Collector* by Jennifer Lanthier and François Thisdale, which is an excellent choice for discussing freedom of expression, and *Woolvs in the Sitee*, by Margaret Wild and illustrated by Anne Spudvilas. The latter book could launch deep discussions on fears and post-apocalyptic settings and how texts can use visual design for impact, along with inventive spellings and unusual fonts, to create an unsettling effect on the reader. Again, critically examining a strong text such as this *through talk* can address any discomfort caused.

## Problem-Based Texts

The texts outlined below present and address problems, including social and moral issues.

*How to Catch a Star*, written and illustrated by Oliver Jeffers, is a simple text with only one or two sentences per page accompanied by appealing child-like drawings in vivid hues. As a problem-based text, it focuses on a young boy's efforts to catch a star. Although it would make a perfect read-aloud for students in Junior Kindergarten to Grade 1, it has a host of fans among B.Ed. students, many of whom have declared it to be one of the most memorable picture books they encountered during their program.

"This book makes my Top 10 list for its beautiful illustrations and because of the determined little boy who shows us all what we can do, especially when we are open to finding things in unexpected places and in unanticipated ways."
— Avery Saunter, B.Ed. student

*The Red Lemon*, which works well for Grades 1 to 4, is another prime example of a text that is problem based. In the story by Bob Staake, the community decides to throw the red lemon as far away as possible (it lands on an island where red lemons grow and a new community flourishes). In Michelle's Grade 3 class, the students formed small groups to discuss alternative solutions. One group of boys decided that the mayor should hold a council meeting to pass a law that things and people who are "different" must be able to stay in the community.

*I Want My Hat Back* by Jon Klassen is the story of a bear who encounters a series of animals and inquires politely about the whereabouts of his hat. The conversations are droll and matter-of-fact, and the illustrations fill us in on key pieces of missing information. The solution to the bear's problem occurs offstage: it seems that the bear sat upon and possibly killed the rabbit who stole his hat.

The ending lends itself to lively discussion about what really happened. In one Kindergarten class, there was a prolonged discussion after the read-aloud. Although some agreed that *the rabbit got what he deserved for stealing the hat*, many of the students adamantly refused to believe that the bear had killed the rabbit. They insisted that the rabbit must have run away. Although Klassen's story is simple, its morally ambiguous ending makes it suitable for dialogue at any age (Kindergarten to Grade 6 especially).

*Four Feet, Two Sandals* is another example of a problem-based text, this time for students in Grades 3 to 8. Again, the problem can be inferred from the title. Movingly told by Karen Lynn Williams and Khadra Mohammed, this story is about friendship and need in extreme conditions, in this case, a refugee camp. Two shoeless girls each find a single plastic sandal and wonder how to solve the problem of who should wear the sandals. Their solutions and ways of sharing are touching and inspiring. The story ends with the girls separating, each keeping a single sandal because "it is good to remember." The book lends itself well to having a grand conversation about key themes and messages.

Here are some key questions, reactions, and responses from Grade 5 students in the context of a read-aloud.

*Contributed by teacher Lorna McKenzie, North Bay, Ontario*

BEFORE: Students look at the cover, which shows two girls with tents and sandy hills in the background, each wearing one yellow sandal with a blue flower:
- "They only have one sandal on each foot! Don't they have any other sandals or shoes to wear?"
- "The title says, *Four Feet, Two Sandals*, so I guess that's it!"
- "Are they camping or do they live there?"

DURING: When refugees are shown scrambling for clothing from the back of a truck:
- "Is that the way they get their clothes?"
- "Don't they have any money?"
  When the girls decide to take turns wearing both sandals:
- "That's better! That's what I would do!"
  When Lina and Feroza discuss family members who were killed in the war:
- "She only has a grandma left? What about if she dies?" *Silence*
  When only Lina and her mother are listed to leave the camp, we stop to talk about what they will do with the sandals:
- "The girl staying, Feroza — she should keep them."
- "But Lina can't go away with bare feet, can she?"
- "Share them!"
- "But what good is that? One sandal each?"

AFTER: In the end, when the girls each keep one sandal to remember:
- "That's because they are friends."
- "Maybe they will meet somewhere later . . ."

As *Four Feet, Two Sandals* illustrates, some problem-based texts present social and moral problems.

A key text in this category is *I Am Not a Number* by Jenny Kay Dupuis and Kathy Kacer, illustrated by Gillian Newland. About a dark part of Canadian history, it is based on the life of co-author Jenny Kay Dupuis's grandmother, Irene Couchie, from Nipissing First Nation in Northern Ontario. The problem is that when Irene attended a residential school, she was treated as a number. Indeed, the eight-year-old was given a number (759) and had her long hair cut. In the face of such treatment, she survived by refusing to forget her name or where she came from. When she returned home for the summer, her parents decided to disobey the unjust law and not have her go back to the school. The story is told in a simple, but powerful way that children can learn from and relate to.

Because of the story's emotional power, responding to this read-aloud through Sketch to Stretch *Plus* (introduced in Chapter 3) is highly effective. In this adaptation of Sketch to Stretch, students may use a drawing to depict their feelings after listening to the story, as well as adding words and graphics. (See the card sample next page.) Talking with a partner or table group occurs before and after the drawings are completed. Whole-group sharing is optional.

Another fascinating text in this category is *Monster Mama* by Liz Rosenberg. This book calls out for talking about the deep themes of mother–child love, otherness (the mother is portrayed as a reclusive "monster" of some sort), what to do with bullies, and how to sit down with your enemies and eat dessert. It is best for children older than age six or seven.

*The art shown here was done by a teacher candidate, Julia Mancuso.*

*As an eight-year-old, Irene Couchie was given the number 759 and not recognized as a unique person.*

## Evocative Texts: Where Visuals Stimulate Conversation

Here, we examine some texts for their ability to evoke stories and themes through effective visual display. When first sharing any of these texts as a read-aloud, be sure to present it slowly. Allow time with each page and for students to interject responses during the viewing (free-flowing commentary). Consider projecting several of the images so that everyone can enjoy the whole and examine in detail.

*The Mysteries of Harris Burdick* by Chris Van Allsburg is iconic in this category. Since it was first published in 1984, it has continued to be read, viewed, discussed, and used as a springboard for storytelling and story writing, particularly in Grades 4 to 6 classrooms. The format is simple but striking: black-and-white and sepia-toned illustrations, one per page, with just a title and a caption to suggest possible stories. Van Allsburg cleverly sets up the series of images with an introduction that claims the publisher was left with only these pictures, titles, and captions after losing track of the author. Whenever this scenario is presented in classrooms (from Grade 4 to B.Ed. levels), students continue to believe the initial story and readily engage in choosing a story to fill in, first orally, and then in writing.

A sequel or update (2011) is *The Chronicles of Harris Burdick*, introduced by Lemony Snicket, with famous authors from Stephen King to Lois Lowry contributing their stories inspired by the original images. Nonetheless, Terry notes: "I continue to introduce the original *Mysteries* to students in my B.Ed. classes, because somehow, most have missed being introduced in their elementary years. Even the most hardened cynics respond at deep levels when conversing and writing about the surrealistic images provided by Van Allsburg."

A group of Terry's teacher candidates designed a lesson plan using the *Mysteries*. They went on a trip outdoors, created mysterious scenes, and took some photographs. They then assigned a title and a caption to match each of their scenes. They wanted models that would inspire students to create a mysterious scene of their own and assign a Van Allsburgian title and caption. A spooky photo, such as the one below, was intended to prompt some interaction and student effort.

*The teacher candidates titled this image "The Mitten Tree," and as their Van Allsburgian caption, asked: "Do you see the shadow of the ice tree?"*

Here is a brief version of the lesson plan designed by a group of four B.Ed. students — Eden Plante, Natalie Ennwah-Akrofi, Suzanne Webster, and Kim Wong.

### The Mysteries of Nipissing University

Begin with Oral Text and Storytelling.

*Before going outdoors:* Read this story and discuss briefly.

One day, Suzanne, Nat, Kim, and Eden went for a walk in the night.
Everything seemed fine
at the time
until they saw something that gave them a great fright.
Something wasn't quite right in the night.
There were eerie sounds in the dark
and funny faces in the bark.
All they had to save them was their flashlight.
The first eerie sign was when they found a black mitten.
It was hanging on a twig.
It was small, not big.
What could have happened? Did he get bitten?
There were claw marks on the trees.
Could it be from the ice bear?
Would he capture a boy? Would he dare?
They hoped they could find him before he were to freeze.

*During the trip:* Kids go for a walk to find clues. They can document using photographs, journal writing, and drawing pictures (bring clipboards); they investigate the area and collect artifacts. They can begin to brainstorm possible stories to link the clues.

*After, back in the classroom:* Students use clues, observations, and brainstorming to discuss and orally create what they think happened (small groups). Tell a story that solves the mystery. Students can create their own endings to the story.

*Next day:* Students, in small groups, set up their own mysteries for their peers to discuss and suggest solutions.

*Imagine a Day* and *Imagine a Night*, both with paintings by Rob Gonsalves and corresponding poems by Sarah L. Thomson, are evocative texts to inspire talk. Each beautiful painting offers intriguing possibilities, along with minimalist poems just four lines after the opener, "Imagine a day . . ." or "Imagine a night . . ." Each pairing can motivate rich conversations in small groups or with the whole class, grand conversation style. For example, imagine the conversation to follow this poem by Terry, modelled on Sarah Thomson's:

*Imagine a moment . . .*
When sky and trees
Join snow-white fields
And they seem to be
looking back at *me!*

Somewhat similarly, *Images of Nature: Canadian Poets and the Group of Seven*, edited by David Booth, displays nature scenes matched with single poems. Each page invites discussion at all levels. When a group of students was asked what they noticed about a painting of trees in the forest, one child said simply, "The shadows. I notice the shadows."

For more detail on how to use
wordless books, please see Chapter 3.

Finally, consider the endless possibilities of wordless books. From David
Wiesner's classic Caldecott Medal winner *Tuesday*, first published in 1991, to the
more recent *Journey* by Aaron Becker, these visual texts offer optimum opportunity for noticing, for predicting, for speculating, and for oohing and aahing.

## Strategies for Use Before, During, and After the Read-Aloud

Here is a summary of oral language strategies related to the use of read-aloud
texts. The strategies allow students to connect to texts, and they encourage
higher-level thinking. As noted earlier, we employ a before-during-after structure
for any read-aloud session to allow students to talk from different perspectives.

### Before: Ways to Warm Up and Stimulate Thinking

- Set up a thought-provoking scene for discussion. For example, before reading *How to Catch a Star*, you could arrange a display of objects relating to
the story, such as a camera, a star pillow, a picnic basket, a soccer ball, and a
picture of a starfish (or a real one, if possible). Display this question: "What
would you do with a star?" Invite open discussion.

   Similarly, before reading *The Most Magnificent Thing*, you could set out an
array of mechanical parts and tools, and ask the class, "What would you make
with these objects?"
- Present an anticipation activity. Display scenes related to a picture book
around the classroom. Invite students to take a gallery walk to music to
examine the scenes and discuss possible stories. Michelle did this with *The
Nutmeg Princess* by Richardo Keens-Douglas, set on a Caribbean island called
the "Isle of Spice." Six scenes from the Caribbean, along with scenes from the
book, were displayed, while Bob Marley music was played. Students walked
and talked in pairs; once they returned to the sharing circle, they related possible stories (Campbell & Hlusek, 2015).
- Show a single visual scene, perhaps a Group of Seven landscape painting or
a Rob Gonsalves painting from *Imagine a Day*. Ask: "What do you notice?
What do you feel?" Students can talk about it with a partner and then share in
the large group. This activity works well prior to viewing any text where the
visuals mainly tell the story or set the atmosphere (as in wordless books).
- Pose oral warm-up questions for students to discuss in small groups. If referring to *17 Things I'm Not Allowed to Do Anymore*, you might ask: "What are
10 things you are not allowed to eat? Which 10 animals are you not allowed
to have for pets? What would you do with an idea?" An appropriate social or
moral problem question might be "What would you do if you had to share
your last $x$ with a friend?" For *The Most Magnificent Thing*, a good warm-up
question is "What can you do when you keep trying to make something and
it just won't work?"

### During: Stop, Think, and Say Something

Stop occasionally to discuss the story so far. Look for natural stopping points
where there is a break in the story, such as a new event or a new character

introduced. Be sure not to stop in the middle of a tense scene or during a quickly moving plot line. Ask: "What are the pictures and words telling us?" Use think-alouds to demonstrate to the students how you think when making meaning from a text, for instance, when making inferences. In books where the words say one thing and the pictures another, you could say aloud what you are thinking as you compare words and images and read between the lines. "As I read this, I am looking at the picture, and I'm thinking, *Hey, what's really going on here?*" If you were reading Jon Klassen's *I Want My Hat Back*, for instance, you might work with a double-page spread where one animal, wearing a red hat, is vehemently denying he has seen the bear's missing hat.

## After: A Range of Response Options

- Implement Sketch to Stretch *Plus*, a strategy explained in detail in Chapter 3. Students respond to texts with time for talking, drawing, writing, and talking again. Texts suitable for Sketch to Stretch approaches include *I Am Not a Number* and *I Am Henry Finch*.
- Hold a town hall discussion, where everyone has a role, including the teacher, who may act as speaker, for example. Other roles may include a mayor, council members, and community activists. They meet to solve a community problem, such as what to do with the red lemon. Plan to spend some time rehearsing roles and setting up the town hall, especially if this is the students' first experience. Assess prior knowledge. Show a video clip of a real city council in action. (Try to find a civil example!)
- Facilitate a grand conversation to discuss the feelings evoked by a book such as *Four Feet, Two Sandals* or *I Am Not a Number*.
- Invite students to make an audio recording with a partner or in a small group to tell a story or episodes in a story where the book, such as *Journey*, is wordless.
- Ask questions of the large group to stimulate real discussion. Begin with open-ended questions, such as "What do you think? How do you feel?" Promote critical thinking through questions like these: "What did the author do or say to lead you to think that? What did the illustrator do to influence your feelings?" Beyond that, you can pose Big Questions connected to life, such as "How can you use your creativity to solve problems in life? What can you do when you lose your cool and want to quit?" *Journey* and *The Most Magnificent Thing* are notably applicable here.

**Encourage Parents to Read Aloud, Too!**

"As parents read with children, they have the opportunity for frequent, sensitively tuned, language-rich interactions that draw children into conversations about books, the world, language and concepts."
— Dickinson, Griffith, Golinkoff, & Hirsh-Pasek, 2012, p. 11

## The Last Word: Students Talk About Read-Alouds

Sometimes, we read a story aloud just to enjoy it. The story is good; the book has marvelous pictures. The aesthetic experience is enough. Sometimes, the read-aloud is an emotional experience, an opportunity to relax, or a way in for some silent pondering afterwards.

For children, the experience can be about just sitting back and listening and imagining. It shouldn't necessarily mean follow-up tasks. Here is what some of Michelle's students said they like about read-alouds:

- "I don't have to read. I get to listen." (Jack, Grade 3)

- "I can understand more when it's a read-aloud. When I read it myself, I don't always understand everything. But when I'm listening to someone read, like my mom or my teacher, I understand more. Also, I don't need to look at the pictures sometimes. I can imagine my own scenes." (Sadi, Grade 4)
- "It's a chance to listen and cool down. It calms me down if I've got too much energy. It cools me down if I'm mad." (Jacob, Grade 4)
- "I can make pictures in my mind and see the story." (Liv, Grade 3)
- "I like listening to stories 'cause I get to show my emotions to it." (Tanya, Grade 4)
- "Stories make me feel calm. I like them because they make me feel good." (Torry, Grade 4)
- "I like when we choose quotes, and then we put them up on the wall." (Sofi, Grade 3)
- "I like when things aren't always what they seem . . ." (Dana, Grade 3)
- "I like the rhyming books. I like to just listen to the sound of the words." (Ali, Grade 3)
- "Sometimes, the stories are funny, sometimes they are sad, sometimes they make you think." (Chris, Grade 3)

"Hearing a stretch of new language in a rereading or a different context will give access to new features of text language. Repeating it in a drama or a refrain might sow seeds that lead to an alternative rule emerging in a child's grammar."
— Marie Clay, 2004, p. 10

With this idea in mind, we will next explore the use of drama in the classroom to extend and expand oral language communication.

---

### Books Worth Talking About: A Selection

#### Picture Books

The emphasis is on ideas and issues worth listening to and talking about, from the humorous to the serious.

*Mainly Primary Grades*

*I Am Henry Finch* by Alexis Deacon, illustrated by Viviane Schwarz

*Asha's Mums* by Rosamund Elwin and Michele Paulse, illustrated by Dawn Lee (also Junior)

*How to Catch a Star* by Oliver Jeffers

*I Want My Hat Back* by Jon Klassen

*My Two Blankets* by Irena Kobald, illustrated by Freya Blackwood

*17 Things I'm Not Allowed to Do Anymore* by Jenny Offill, illustrated by Nancy Carpenter

*The Most Magnificent Thing* by Ashley Spires

*Ooko* by Esmé Shapiro

*The Red Lemon* by Bob Staake

*Mainly Junior–Intermediate Grades*

*Images of Nature* edited by David Booth

*I Am Not a Number* by Jenny Kay Dupuis and Kathy Kacer, illustrated by Gillian Newland

*So, What's It Like to Be a Cat?* by Karla Kuskin, illustrated by Betsy Lewin

*And Tango Makes Three* by Justin Richardson and Peter Parnell, illustrated by Henry Cole

*Imagine a Day* by Sarah L. Thomson, illustrated by Rob Gonsalves

*Imagine a Night* by Sarah L. Thomson, illustrated by Rob Gonsalves

*The Mysteries of Harris Burdick* by Chris Van Allsburg

*Four Feet, Two Sandals* by Karen Lynn Williams and Khadra Mohammed, illustrated by Doug Chayka

*For Older Students (Grades 6 to 8)*

*The Watertower* by Gary Crew, illustrated by Steven Woolman

*The Stamp Collector* by Jennifer Lanthier, illustrated by François Thisdale

*Woolvs in the Sitee* by Margaret Wild, illustrated by Anne Spudvilas

**Wordless Books**

The images in wordless books can stimulate conversation. (See Chapter 3 for more on the use of this type of book.)

*Journey* by Aaron Becker

*The Boys* by Jeff Newman

*Bluebird* by Bob Staake

*Tuesday* by David Wiesner

# 6

............................................................................................................

# Using Drama to Enhance Oral Communication

*As play happens, language learning expands and multiplies uses of images, music, dance, drama and poetry.*

*— Shirley Brice Heath, 2013, p. 189*

*I liked doing our performance of the Three Billy Goats.*
*I was the Troll under the bridge we made from chairs.*
*We all said the last lines together.*
*Everyone clapped. It felt great.*

*— Larry, Grade 3 student*

This chapter explores how talk takes centre stage in dramatic expression. In particular, it considers which classroom talk activities partner most effectively with drama. It also addresses how we can use these activities to enhance oral communication, both listening and speaking.

Drama in the classroom is about learning out loud. Since drama involves *speaking* along with the physical expression of spoken thoughts and feelings, literacy and language learning are natural partners with it. As Larry Swartz puts it, "drama promotes literacy growth, and literacy growth promotes drama exploration" (2014, p. 6).

Dramatic expression is a natural human impulse evident in the early years of childhood. We know that dramatic play contributes to the cognitive development of young children (Piaget, 1962), but it goes beyond intellectual benefits. In a position paper, the National Association for the Education of Young Children states, "high-level dramatic play produces documented cognitive, social, and emotional benefits" (Copple & Bredekamp, 2009, p. 15). As any Kindergarten teacher can testify, children come to school knowing how to engage in *pretend play*. Teachers design their classrooms accordingly with drama and socio-dramatic play centres.

*How can teachers fully capitalize on children's innate enthusiasm for engaging in drama activities in Kindergarten and the years beyond?* This chapter explores this question by delving into everyday drama activities that can be seamlessly integrated into the life of the classroom throughout the elementary years. The focus is not on the sort of public performance epitomized by the high-school musical;

"In pretend play, children use language and thinking skills to compare, plan, investigate materials, problem solve, experiment, negotiate, evaluate."
— Ontario Ministry of Education, 2010–2011, p. 70

it is on promoting the use of dramatic expression as part of daily learning. The benefits are many. This chapter focuses mainly on the *literacy out loud* links, or links between drama and enhanced oral communication.

## Not Quiet on the Set! Drama Produces Better Communication

Strong research evidence links experiences in drama with improved literacy, including oral communication. One well-known researcher in oral language development is Shirley Brice Heath. Heath studied at-risk middle-childhood and adolescent learners who "participated in performances in the arts." She found that they made strong progress in language and literacy skills in general and that this was noticeably evident when the students were in high school. She also found a significant relationship between time spent in "arts learning environments," such as studios, theatres, and galleries, and the development of "fluent talk" about their endeavors (2004, p. 338).

Although Heath initially examined the links between exposure to the arts and acquisition of oral and written language, she went on to find evidence of links between enjoyment in the arts and other forms of learning:

> It appears artists see learning as ways of solving problems that may arise,
> and because much of the work of art involves casting the self forward
> and needing to anticipate variables or circumstances that may affect that
> performance, anticipatory problem seeing and problem solving have high
> appeal. (2004, p. 340)

Therefore, in addition to enhancing oral communication, involvement in drama (and in other arts) offers related benefits, such as the fostering of problem-solving abilities.

When we think of the social context of collaborative drama activities and observe our students organizing and rehearsing, this finding makes perfect sense. Even when the drama activity involves little or no speech — for example, in mime or tableau work — the efforts of group members getting ready to present require effective use of oral communication skills. The research evidence suggests that this is one reason for improvements in oral language use.

Research with students in Kindergarten and Grade 1 supports Heath's findings. Greenfader and Brouillette (2013) found that using drama and movement with young English language learners helped to boost their oral language skills. They describe one Kindergarten teacher who uses drama and teacher modelling to promote language learning. Here is an example of his warm-up technique:

> "Actors, five point position, please!" The kindergartners jump to attention,
> standing with hands at their sides, heads high, feet together. Most of the
> children have limited English skills, yet they follow along easily because
> their teacher demonstrates as he speaks. (p. 174)

Drama activities usually involve both voice and movement; the teacher's physical modelling helps students when they are learning a new language or new words. For all learners who may be striving to become orally confident, drama provides opportunities for low-risk, small-group interactions, whereby quiet or reluctant speakers can feel comfortable practising oral language skills.

As noted earlier, oral communication (along with reading, writing, and media literacy) is a key literacy strand. The Ontario Ministry of Education (2006, p. 9), for one, states that the general expectations for learning in this strand include the ability "to use speaking skills and strategies appropriately to communicate with different audiences for a variety of purposes."

Two dimensions are particularly pertinent to dramatic expression:

1. Using *vocal effects*, including tone, pace, pitch, and volume, and using them appropriately to help communicate meaning (e.g., increasing volume to emphasize important points or be heard by a large audience)
2. Becoming aware of *non-verbal cues*, including facial expression, gestures, and eye contact, and using them in oral communication appropriately and with sensitivity towards cultural differences to help convey their meaning

Helping students develop their use of vocal effects and non-verbal cues can be integral to many daily classroom activities, from conversations to choral speaking. Activities intended to enhance oral language proficiency while infusing the dramatic dimension are explored throughout this chapter. All the drama activities described are occasions for practising and demonstrating the following oral language skills:

- speaking at a volume appropriate to the audience, and in keeping with the meaning of the words spoken
- enunciating words clearly
- speaking fluently with expression
- using vocal effects, such as tone, pace, and pitch
- using non-verbal cues, such as facial expressions, eye contact, and gestures

*We need to deal w/this in BL Doc.*

# Choral Speaking — No Two Oral Interpretations Alike

Larry Swartz describes *choral speaking* as an opportunity for students to "read aloud such texts as rhymes and poems by assigning parts among group members. By working with peers to read aloud poems on a particular theme or topic or by a single poet, students take part in a creative activity that involves experimentation with voice, sound, gesture, and movement. *Because of these variations, no two oral interpretations of a single poem are alike*" (2014, p. 17, emphasis added).

We found that last statement to be true when we used a poem version of "The Three Billy Goats Gruff" to implement choral speaking then dramatization in Michelle's classroom. The entire process described below took about 90 minutes.

## Working with "The Three Billy Goats Gruff"

We began by asking for a student to retell the story because not everyone in the class was familiar with it. Several students volunteered; Ali was familiar with the story "from Grade 1."

1. *Whole-class choral speaking:* Our story-poem version of the tale was projected for all to see (a line-master version appears on page 86). We then set about familiarizing the students with the story-poem, which is partly chanted and partly sung, by using "repeat after me" or echo reading two to

---

**Drama-Related Strategies**

The following strategies, discussed in this chapter, can be integrated into daily classroom activities:

- choral speaking and dramatization
- warm-ups involving drama
- dramatic play centres
- minimal scripts
- rich use of nursery rhymes
- interviewing in role
- question-and-answer dialogues
- use of mentor texts
- tableau creation

This story-poem is suitable for Grades 1 to 4. Terry has used it successfully with a Grade 1 class, where the process began with choral reading over several days and culminated in a whole-class performance in which four students performed the actions in role as the troll and the three goats, and the rest of the class narrated the lines in unison. In Michelle's Grade 3–4 class, the sequence involved moving from choral speaking to small-group dramatizations.

four lines at a time. After we tapped into prior learning and used echo reading, the whole group participated in a unison choral reading of the entire story-poem. We all kept the beat by snapping our fingers in 4/4 time (**strong** *weak* medium *weak*).

2. *Small-group choral speaking focused on experimenting:* We divided the class into three groups, each with about eight members. Each group was assigned part of the poem and given a copy of it with their part highlighted. Groups discussed what kinds of voices they should use and tried out their parts with exaggerated voices. One group, representing the little goat, was quiet and high. A second group represented the middle goat with medium volume and lower tones. The third group, representing both the biggest goat and the troll, took the loudest and lowest parts.

3. *Whole story-poem by whole class:* The teacher then narrated the whole story-poem, and each group came in on cue, demonstrating its oral interpretation. This exercise helped the students warm up for their work in small groups using the entire poem.

4. *Dramatization in small groups:* The class then formed groups of three to five students to experiment with their interpretation of the story-poem. Each group was given one copy of the poem. They were instructed to continue to explore using their voices for the various parts, this time preparing the entire poem for presentation by everyone in the group. Michelle reminded them of the posted success criteria they had co-created earlier in the year for effective speaking and listening (see the anchor chart below). The students were encouraged to find their own way to rehearse and prepare the story-poem for performance. For example, they might each take a role: narrator, little, middle, or big billy goat, and the troll. Some groups decided to double up roles, especially for the louder parts, such as the troll. For example, one group working well together rehearsed with two boys under the table playing the troll. That same group had a member who spontaneously took on the role of director, encouraging the narrator to slow down and speak clearly and directing the "goats" to cross over to the other side of the table at the right time.

**Punch, Pause, and Paint**

One way to add spice to a chorally spoken poem is to encourage students to annotate their poems or scripts to indicate where they will

- *punch* words, by adding emphasis
- *pause* to adjust the pace
- *paint* words, by using expression and tone

(O'Connor, 2004)

---

### Speaking and Listening Anchor Chart for Presentations

√   I speak loudly enough so that everyone can hear me.
√   I speak clearly so that everyone can understand me.
√   I contribute to my group when preparing to present.
√   I show support for my peers by listening respectfully to their presentations.

---

*Observations*

Although one group stayed sitting at a table and used just their voices and sound effects (banging a drum for the biggest goat), all other groups used *movement* as well, although we had not explicitly mentioned the use of actions. Two groups used improvised props and movement to depict the goats crossing the bridge and the troll popping his head out from under the bridge.

"I liked doing 'The Three Billy Goats.' I liked that we got to pick our own groups and choose our own parts, and we did it fairly. I played the little goat, *so I got to talk like this* [high voice]. I liked that we all used fun voices."
— Alisha, Grade 4

All groups incorporated the use of sound in their presentations: two used classroom drums, and others used tabletops to thump out the biggest goat crossing the bridge.

We noted that, although the students had scripts, after the first rehearsal (and chorally speaking earlier with the whole class), many could recite their parts from memory. That freed them to concentrate on using voice, sound, and movement to dramatize the poem.

Within 30 minutes, they were ready to present. Parts were chanted individually, in tandem, and at times in unison. Some groups used props such as tables, chairs, and drums. Some used movement such as physically crawling across a chair bridge. Others used exaggeratedly high or low voices, and loud and soft voices. Sometimes, the script was referred to; at other times, lines were recited from memory.

The final group to present recited the last lines of the poem in unison:

> Then that Billy Goat inflicted pain,
> And the mean old troll . . .
> was never heard of again.

They then raised their joined hands and bowed in traditional curtain-call fashion. There was applause all around.

As Larry Swartz had predicted, no two interpretations were alike.

*Assessment*

The group presentations were videotaped, and a checklist was used to record participation and use of voice (e.g., pitch, volume, enunciation). Good models include "Assessment: Choral Speaking and Dramatization," on page 87, which Michelle uses, and the one on page 25 in Larry Swartz's *Dramathemes*, fourth edition. Observational notes were kept on group collaboration and discussion.

A final large-group discussion was held for peer- and self-assessment. The class referred to its anchor chart for presentations (see page 78).

"I like the way we made a bridge with two chairs and I was the troll under the chair-bridge. We all said the last lines together. Everyone clapped. It felt great."
— Larry, Grade 3

**Managing Stops and Starts**

To help manage the start or stop of any drama presentation, especially small group, you can use "Lights, Camera, Action." The class says "Lights," and everyone quickly opens and closes hands at shoulder height once. Members then say "Camera" and make a circular movement away from the body as if reeling a film; then, everyone says, "Action!" With top hand extended, everyone claps down on the bottom hand, miming a film action bar. As for "Freeze!" both hands are open and extended, palms down.

An alternative approach is to use a drum, a bell, or sticks with different beats to signify go and stop.

Be sure to practise these signals first.

---

### Selected Poems Suitable for Choral Speaking and Dramatization

*Doctor Knickerbocker and Other Rhymes* edited by David Booth, illustrated by Maryann Kovalski (Grades 1 to 6)
*You Read to Me, I'll Read to You: Very Short Stories to Read Together* by Mary Ann Hoberman, illustrated by Michael Emberley (Grades 2 to 4)
"The Spider and the Fly" by Mary Howitt (Grades 4 to 8)
"Alligator Pie" by Dennis Lee (in *Alligator Pie*) (Kindergarten to Grade 8)
*So Cool* by Dennis Lee, illustrated by Maryann Kovalski (Grades 4 to 8)
"Today" by Jean Little (in *Hey World, Here I Am!*) (Grades 4 to 6)
"The Highwayman" by Alfred Noyes
"Sick" and "Whatif" by Shel Silverstein (in *Where the Sidewalk Ends*) (Grades 3 to 6)

# Everyday Drama Activities

The following activities can be used during the classroom literacy block and, in some cases, can be integrated into content-area instructional time. Most can be used in Junior Kindergarten through to Grade 8, with appropriate adaptations as needed.

## Warm-ups and Focusing Strategies Using Drama

**Variation on a Silent Cheer**

The student raises hands on either side of the head with three fingers showing, mouths the word *wow* as one hand is raised with three fingers, like a W, then the mouth is opened like an O, and then the other hand is displayed with three fingers as a W. This is a good management strategy for showing appreciation for a performance, an alternative to loud cheering.

*Focusing Fingerplay:* For Junior Kindergarten to Grade 2, this brief whole-class fingerplay is useful as a focusing strategy immediately before large-group instruction of any kind, from a read-aloud to a science demonstration. Students sit cross-legged, say each line aloud, and make the appropriate gestures:

> I relax and focus. (*thumb to self, hands on lap*)
> I gather in the good. (*gather with hands*)
> I push away the bad. (*hands open-palmed, pushing straight ahead*)
> I celebrate the joy all around me. (*raising both hands, waving a silent cheer*)

*Voice Warm-ups:* Students form groups of four, members standing in a circle, facing in. One word at a time, they go around the circle saying, "To be or not to be." Next, they say, "Zig-zag-zog," one word at a time, one person at a time. Then, it's "Slip-slap-slop." Finally, they say: "Bing-Bang-Boing."

Variations include speaking with exaggerated pronunciation, saying words loudly but without shouting, singing, whispering, speaking slowly, or speaking quickly. Students can also vary pitch, intonation, and emphasis.

Invite feedback from the students on how they must use their facial muscles, lips, and tongues to pronounce these nonsense words. Ask them to comment on how variations change the feelings evoked. These warm-ups work well for students in Grades 3 to 8.

*Mime Strategies:* Using pre-rehearsed start and stop signals (e.g., saying "Action" to start and "Freeze" to stop), the teacher or a student director gives directions, like these: "climb up the stairs," "try to whistle," "walk on the moon," "walk as if you're a queen or king wearing a crown," "cut a ribbon," "put up an umbrella," "walk in the rain," "stagger in the wind," and "twirl your umbrella." Warm-ups for movement are best done in an open space.

**Literacy Extensions**

The movement activity can be used to reinforce knowledge about verbs. Invite the students to add to the list of directions using verbs. Similarly, for the facial expression warm-ups, students can add to the list of emotions and describe related situations.

The teacher or student director can also call for "quick change" emotions, where students show emotion through facial expression. Students respond to prompts such as "Show me mad because you dropped your ice cream," ". . . sad because your friend is moving away," ". . . surprise because you got an A."

## Dramatic Play Centres

Primarily used in Kindergarten and early primary grades, learning centres that focus on dramatic inquiry and exploration can also be set up in any elementary grade.

In socio-dramatic play centres (JK to Grade 1), children engage in spontaneous role-play as they enact real-life situations. For example, a dramatic play centre can be transformed into a flower shop, a hospital, a restaurant or a coffee shop, or an art gallery. When their creation is driven by the students' interests, centre settings and scenarios offer great opportunities for dramatic play. They require research on the part of the students: What types of flowers to sell? How do people act in this setting? What types of people go to this place? What do they say, and how do they say it? *Talk is essential in these learning situations.*

Drama centres for students in Grades 3 to 8 can be set up for dramatic response activities following a read-aloud. For example, in Terry's B.Ed. classroom, teacher candidates have created activities based on Métis Canadian author David Bouchard's *Nokum Is My Teacher,* a dialogue between a Cree boy and his Nokum (grandmother) about the values of schooling and literacy inside and outside their culture. The book comes with a CD, the story told in both English and in Cree. The teacher candidates suggested designing a drama centre featuring the book and a device for listening to the CD. Pairs of students could listen to the story, refer to the book, discuss, and then re-enact the dialogue in role, using words from the text. The centre could provide a shawl for Nokum and a talking stick for the boy.

As far as extensions go, students could use materials provided at the centre to write a letter in role from the perspective of a character: Nokum, the boy, a teacher, or any of the uncles who are mentioned in the story. They could write the letter as though addressing another character. If desired, students could rehearse their written letters orally, using props or costumes, and present their writing in role during sharing time. Another option is for students to perform their letter as a *monologue,* the text memorized. Terry's students presented these in the university classroom, and many implemented their ideas in junior- and intermediate-level classrooms when on placement.

## Using Minimal Scripts for Maximum Effect

Minimal scripts, both teacher prepared and student created, offer rich opportunities to explore dramatic expression and enhance everyday conversations. Short scripts can be expressed in different ways to explore the use of voice, volume, pitch, timing, gestures, emotions, facial expression, and movement.

As Larry Swartz (2014) writes in *Dramathemes,* "Minimal scripts of two to six lines are significant sources for students to explore the fundamental elements of good theatre" (p. 144). By adapting the subject matter of the script, this strategy can be used by students in Grades 1 through 8.

In partners, students can experiment with saying a few lines aloud in various ways. One person is A, and the other is B. Students can also think about and discuss who is speaking (characters), where the conversation is taking place (the setting or scene), and what the background story might be. They can improvise continuations of the conversation, or use the minimal script as an ending. This sample is found in Swartz (2014, p. 144):

A. What happened to you?
B. I'd rather not talk about it.
A. Why won't you tell me?
B. OK, but promise not to tell anybody.

Students can be prompted to say the lines in a variety of ways, including quickly or slowly, in a whisper, as if talking on a telephone, and in a sing-song voice. A can say the lines angrily, while B says them calmly. A and B can sit back to back. B can show no interest in what A is saying. And so on.

Lev Vygotsky writes that play is the work of children: that children learn best through play. As they role-play being literate adults, children are functioning at a high level of what Vygotsky terms *proximal development.*

"Participants in socio-dramatic play communicate with each other using language and symbolic gestures to describe and extrapolate from familiar experiences, and to imagine and create new stories. Socio-dramatic play supports children's self-regulation and increases their potential to learn as they engage with the people and resources in their environment (Pascal, 2009a)."
— Ontario Ministry of Education, 2016b, p. 20

For several years, Terry has introduced the practice of using minimal scripts to teacher candidates, having them say the same four lines in many different ways. She comments: "They always enjoy it and comment on what a simple, low-risk, but richly engaging activity it is."

**It's not what you say. It's how you say it.**

For authoritative information on minimal scripts, as well as the use of nursery rhymes and more, be sure to check out *Dramathemes,* fourth edition, by Larry Swartz.

## Contagious Conversations

Students from Grades 1 to 8 can apply a strategy from improv drama which involves starting with an assigned opening line. Each participant (except the last) must add a line beginning with the word *and*. This activity, best conducted in a circle, can be small-group work. The idea is that the word *and* builds on the first person's spoken words and ideas, and keeps the conversation flowing. By contrast, the word *but* tends to put an end to the interchange. Student A says the first line, then taps B, who must continue, beginning with the word *and*. Then B taps C, and so on. Direct students to keep the talk going until they hear a signal, when the last speaker must start the final sentence with the word *but*. Here is an example, where the teacher provides the first line:

A.  Cats are amazing creatures . . .
B.  And they make great pets
C.  And they are furry, clever, and cuddly
D.  And they know how to keep themselves clean
E.  But they sometimes kill birds.

# Exploring the Potential of Nursery Rhymes

**Recommended Resources**

*Sing a Song of Mother Goose* by Barbara Reid
*Here Comes Mother Goose,* edited by Iona Opie, illustrated by Rosemary Wells

Nursery rhymes are condensed stories. They lend themselves well to dramatic interpretation and expression because a whole story is there in just a few lines. The words roll off one's tongue because they have been polished into poetic pearls over years of oral transmission. They come from many cultural sources and are available in the public domain for easy access.

These activities are appropriate for students from Kindergarten to Grade 8.

- *Change a line of nursery rhyme back to front.* Take, for example, "Mary had a little lamb," changing the last word each time, as in "Mary had a little rhinoceros; Mary had a furry rhinoceros . . ." This can be done with the whole class in Kindergarten to Grade 2 or in small groups in Grades 3 to 4.
- *Recite rhymes with actions.* "I'm a Little Teapot" works well as a model. Students can also add actions to match the words of nursery rhymes such as "Jack and Jill," "Humpty Dumpty," "Miss Polly Had a Dolly," and "Two Little Blue Birds."

   Teach "I'm a Little Teapot" with visuals and modelling, followed by introducing other rhymes for adding actions. Once students have the idea, this activity can become part of a dramatic play centre.
- *Change the last line.* A nursery rhyme can be given a humorous or incongruent ending, as these examples indicate.

   *Primary*
   I'm a little teapot, short and stout (*stand with tummy pushed out*)
   Here is my handle (*place one hand on hip for handle*)
   Here is my . . . (*place second hand on hip, and look from handle to handle in surprise*)
   GOOD HEAVENS! I'M A SUGAR BOWL!

   *Junior*
   Hey diddle diddle, the cat and the fiddle
   The cow jumped over the moon

The little dog laughed to see such sport
And the rap star threw down his cell phone. *(mime having phone to ear and then throwing it down)*

You might suggest other rhymes for students to create new endings to, using modern references. Students can work in partners or in small groups.

- *Explore character through interviews.* Working with a nursery rhyme, students can explore characters and what happened to them before and after the events of the rhyme. For example, what happened to Jack and Jill after they fell down the hill? Students could find out more about them by role-playing interviews. Two students could be in role as Jack and as Jill with other students playing celebrity entertainment journalists (Grades 3 to 6).
- *Role-play characters in new settings.* Students in Grades 4 to 6 can role-play well-known characters in specific settings and imagine what they might say. For example, Jack and Jill might be at the foot of Mount Everest, and Jill is trying to talk Jack into climbing it. What will they say? How will they act?
- *Re-enact a nursery rhyme as a crime scene.* For example, the class could dramatize the story of the Queen of Hearts, whose tarts were stolen. *The Top Secret Files of Mother Goose!* by Gabby Gosling is a hilarious text to use to introduce using nursery rhyme characters as criminal suspects:

> There's been a crime at the castle. The Queen of Hearts' tarts have vanished, leaving Her Majesty hungry and cranky. With only a few clues, will Mother Goose, Chief Detective of Nursery Rhyme Crime, be able to solve this crumby case? Join Detective Goose as she questions all the usual suspects, collecting a file of Top Secret information. (Goodreads, 2017)

## Asking Questions, Composing Answers

Two essential skills for *learning out loud* are asking well-designed questions and composing effective answers. Since use of these skills often arises in the context of conversations and interviews, practising the skills using drama is a natural way to improve their quality. The skills are then transferable to writing.

### Interviewing in Role

In addition to the role-play that students can engage in while exploring nursery rhymes, they can turn to other sources, such as picture books and novels, to gain ideas on interviewing in role. This technique can be used in curricular areas such as science, social studies, and history, where pairs must research the animal or person being interviewed.

In the picture book *So, What's It Like to Be a Cat?* a boy interviews a cat about what it really thinks and feels. After a read-aloud, students can use the book as a model for interviewing various animals. In partners, one student can play the role of an animal and the second student can serve as interviewer. Since the cat in the book has been anthropomorphized into a very articulate (and amusing) interviewee, students can then use the questions from the text as sample questions to interview a classmate, seeking to find out more about the person being interviewed. This activity is suitable for students in Grades 2 to 8.

Somewhat like the Queen of Hearts activity above, students (especially in Grades 4 to 6) can experience *Abel's Island*, by William Steig, as a crime scene. In the novel, a gentleman mouse is separated from his wife when they are picnicking, and a sudden storm blows in. Abel is lost or *has disappeared* for one year. You may want to set up the scene of the crime as an abruptly deserted picnic, outdoors if possible. Have some students role-play detectives interviewing suspects and witnesses, or play reporters (TV, radio, newspaper) interviewing witnesses. To provide guidance for role-playing, sample TV or radio clips, along with newspaper clippings, can be used to give the students models for the kind of language and types of questions detectives and reporters (and witnesses) are likely to use.

## Question-and-Answer Dialogues

### Primary Grades

Use models found in nursery rhymes that begin with questions. These include "Mary, Mary, quite contrary, how does your garden grow?" and "Pussycat, Pussycat, where have you been?" Have students recite the familiar rhymes and then orally compose their own questions and answers with a partner.

You could also use picture books written in question-and-answer format. These include *Stella, Queen of the Snow* and other Stella and Sam books by Marie-Louise Gay; *I Want My Hat Back* by Jon Klassen; and *How Do Dinosaurs Say Goodnight?* by Jane Yolen. There are also question-based nonfiction texts, such as *What Do You Do with a Tail Like That?* by Steve Jenkins and Robin Page.

Have students create their own question-and-answer dialogues modelled on a chosen text. For nonfiction topics, time and resources need to be provided for research. For an extension, students could compose question-and-answer dialogues in rhyme, for example: "What is it like to be a bat? I can only imagine that."

### Junior–Intermediate Grades

The art of dramatizing question-and-answer dialogues has links to *inquiry learning*. Inquiry begins with the students' own questions, and the possibilities can be explored through drama prior to beginning research. For more on this, check out *Drama for Learning* by Dorothy Heathcote and Gavin Bolton (1994).

Begin with texts that inspire questions, for example, Chris Van Allsburg's *The Stranger* and *The Wretched Stone*; and historical and biographical texts such as *Hana's Suitcase* by Karen Levine and Maxine Trottier's *Terry Fox: A Story of Hope*.

---

### Mentor Texts as Models

Remember to use texts that model dramatic conversations and rich oral language, and can form the basis for the drama-related strategies. Many texts can serve as models for oral language structures, such as dialogue and conversation, and are good sources for vocabulary enrichment.

Mentor texts that model oral language forms have useful applications to writing as well. Select texts that model vibrant personal voice in speech. For example, you may want to share the whimsically illustrated text *Ooko*, by Esmé Shapiro, with your class. A fox who is seeking a friend speaks in first-person statements, thus revealing its thoughts and feelings. Bear in mind texts that model the various purposes of language, too. *Don't Let the Pigeon Drive the Bus*, *Don't Let the Pigeon Stay Up Late*, and the other popular pigeon books by mo willems, for example, model the arts of persuasive speech and persuasive writing. First saying the words aloud from various texts provides rehearsal for students to create and write their own dialogue.

---

## Tableaux with a Twist

A tableau is a frozen scene, or still action shot, created by a group using their bodies to project a visual view of an activity or event from a story or a passage from a poem. Usually, there is no speaking unless a narrator is assigned. It is not the most obvious way to promote oral communication, but it can.

As a teacher educator, Kristen Ferguson (2014) shares with teacher candidates how to dramatize a poem through tableau activities. A favorite text for Grades 4 to 6 is Leroy F. Jackson's "Away to the River," beginning as follows:

> Away to the river, away to the wood,
> While the grasses are green and the berries are good!
> Where the locusts are scraping their fiddles and bows,
> And the bees keep a-coming wherever one goes.

Here are three of her suggestions for creating "tableaux with a twist." In particular, note "What Am I Thinking?"

- In the "What Am I Thinking?" activity, students, while frozen, make a statement or ask a question about what their animal, character, or object might be thinking while it is playing by the river.
- Students can create a chronological series of tableaux to sequence the beginning, middle, and end of the poem. The talk is in the preparation.
- As a narrator reads aloud the poem, students can act out or pantomime a line or two of the poem and then freeze to create a tableau for that moment. For instance, students could pantomime being the bees at the riverside and then freeze as they surround the narrator.

## What to Strive For in the Drama Classroom

Part of being a literate person is the ability to orally communicate effectively. Engagement in drama activities creates multiple opportunities for students to practise and perform oral communication skills. Here are some ideas to keep in mind when introducing drama activities into your classroom.

- Think about what the classroom environment should look like and feel like (both physical space and free expression).
- Think about which skills and attitudes should be present for effective drama to take place.
- Ensure a safe environment for risk taking: establish *trust*.
- Emphasize the importance of maintaining *focus*.
- Emphasize teamwork.
- Focus on use of voice and movement.
- Explore trying another person's perspective.
- Encourage imagination and creativity.
- Encourage collaborative problem-solving.
- Maintain an atmosphere of fun.
- Provide plenty of time for practice and rehearsal.
- Capitalize on the literacy links between drama and oral language experience, vocabulary building, and communication skills by integrating drama daily.

# The Three Billy Goats Gruff

*(For shared reading, choral reading, chanting, or singing in 4/4 time)*

A long time ago in a fairy tale, there lived three billy goats named Gruff.
One was little, **and one was middle, and One Was TOUGH!**
Under the bridge lived a mean old troll.
He gobbled up people when he lost control.

[*High, tiny voice*]: Trippety-trap, trippety-trap, trippety, trippety, trippety trap.
***WHO'S THAT TRIP-TROPPING OVER MY BRIDGE?***
It's I! It's I! It's only I!
***THEN I'M COMING TO GOBBLE YOU UP!***
Oh, no! Don't eat me!
I'm just the littlest one of the three!
Then that troll, well bless my soul,
that mean old troll, he lost control,
and then he let that billy goat pass
— over the bridge — and onto the grass.

[*Medium voice*]: Trippety-trap, trippety-trap, trippety, trippety, trippety trap.
***WHO'S THAT TRIP-TROPPING OVER MY BRIDGE?***
It's I! It's I! It's only I!
***THEN I'M COMING TO GOBBLE YOU UP!***
Oh, no! Don't eat me!
I'm just the **middlest** one of the three!
Then that troll, well bless my soul,
that mean old troll, he lost control,
and then he let that billy goat pass
— over the bridge — and onto the grass.

[*Big and loud*]: **TRIPPETY-TROP! BANG! BANG! TRIPPETY-TROP! BANG! BANG!**
***WHO'S THAT TRIP-TROPPING OVER MY BRIDGE?***
**IT'S I! IT'S I! IT'S I!**
***THEN I'M COMING TO GOBBLE YOU UP!***
OH, NO! YOU WON'T GET ME! I'M THE BIGGEST GRUFF AND I'M MIGHTY TOUGH!
Then that billy goat inflicted pain,
and the mean old troll . . .
was never heard of again!

Pembroke Publishers ©2017 *Literacy Out Loud* by Terry Anne Campbell and Michelle E. McMartin ISBN 978-1-55138-323-1

# Assessment: Choral Speaking and Dramatization

Name: _____   Date: _____

| Student Actions | Always | Sometimes | Not Yet |
| --- | :---: | :---: | :---: |
| Participates in whole-group speaking | ☐ | ☐ | ☐ |
| Participates in small-group speaking | ☐ | ☐ | ☐ |
| Takes on an individual role in drama | ☐ | ☐ | ☐ |
| Uses voice appropriate to role | ☐ | ☐ | ☐ |
| Contributes to group discussion when preparing presentation | ☐ | ☐ | ☐ |
| Listens to peers and speaks in role at the appropriate time | ☐ | ☐ | ☐ |
| Uses appropriate volume | ☐ | ☐ | ☐ |
| Uses appropriate pacing | ☐ | ☐ | ☐ |
| Changes pitch according to role | ☐ | ☐ | ☐ |
| Enunciates words clearly | ☐ | ☐ | ☐ |
| Experiments with use of voice, sound, and movement | ☐ | ☐ | ☐ |
| Encourages participation of all group members | ☐ | ☐ | ☐ |
| Shows support for presentations of other groups | ☐ | ☐ | ☐ |
| Participates in final large-group discussion | ☐ | ☐ | ☐ |

NOTES:

Pembroke Publishers ©2017 *Literacy Out Loud* by Terry Anne Campbell and Michelle E. McMartin ISBN 978-1-55138-323-1

# 7

# Speaking from the Heart: Storytelling

*[handwritten: Bl. Doc + writing class? ⊛]*

*We humans are storytelling animals. The drive to story is basic in all people, and exists in all cultures. Stories shape our lives and our culture — we cannot seem to live without them.*

— *David Booth and Bob Barton, 2000, p. 7*

*I love seeing the look on other people's faces when they hear my story. I like getting help from my friends. It helps make the story better.*

— *Jaimee, Grade 5 student*

Anyone who can talk can tell stories. Stories are an integral part of life and learning. We pass along the latest events of our daily lives, expressing ourselves with our voices, our pauses, and our gestures. Listeners lend their ears to the speaker, visualizing the scene in their minds. They may be reminded of a similar tale from their lives or a story they encountered through reading or listening to a storyteller. In these ways, children learn oral language skills in many settings. We can use these naturally learned skills and build on them in our classrooms.

This chapter explores possible classroom practices pertaining to oral storytelling, both formal and informal. In its traditional form, the art of storytelling uses the spoken word, sometimes accompanied by music, movement, and gesture, to communicate a story to a live audience. Oral storytelling in its informal, conversational forms is worth exploring in the classroom, as well. In all its forms, storytelling is notable for the way that listeners create their own visual images, thus co-creating the story with the storyteller.

## Cultural Considerations in Story Selection

Since stories come from many sources, both oral and in print, let us first address a few important cultural issues affecting how we select stories for our classrooms.

When selecting stories for reading aloud or telling orally, we need to bear in mind that the cultural origins of the stories are relevant. The issue of *cultural appropriation* arises most dramatically when authors or filmmakers from one culture use material from another culture to tell a story *as if from their point of view*. In the context of the classroom, we need to be aware of this issue, particu-larly when telling unpublished stories from another person's culture and when engaging in follow-up activities, such as making dream catchers, when they are taken out of their rightful context. On the other hand, there is a wealth of pub-lished stories that can contribute to our *cultural appreciation* for the wonder-ful diversity found in our schools and neighborhoods and around the world. As educators, we want our students to be exposed to and to appreciate stories from many backgrounds. Through these many tales, we can learn about differences, but also about the many things we share as human beings.

## Showing Respect

Here, each of us shares an individual perspective on cultural appropriation and story choice.

"As a teacher, you need to understand the culture of your classroom," says Michelle. "Know your students and know your families. Take time to educate yourself. Invite members from cultural communities into your classroom to create mutual respect and understanding. Honor traditions. I remember when I was a student in Grade 5, my French teacher was Jewish. He set up the classroom to celebrate Hanukkah with us. This was a very impactful experience for us as students to understand and respect another culture.

"Our Community Circle is grounded in Indigenous teachings," she continued. "Our classroom rules are based on the Grandfather Teachings, the most impor-tant one being respect. That respect transcends to the choices I make in choosing stories to share with my class."

"When choosing stories to work with in the classroom, we should consider the cultural sources of the stories," says Terry. "In Michelle's community setting, for example, there are a significant number of students with First Nations and Métis heritage. Teachers in her school and district board in Northern Ontario often invite guests from the Nipissing First Nation reserve to tell stories from their Ojibwe culture and to talk about their beliefs and practices. Non-Indigenous teachers would not dream of engaging in activities such as making drums or dream catchers without the presence of those who rightfully own these practices. The same goes for telling their unpublished stories.

"When using *published* traditional stories from Indigenous peoples, it is respectful to make every effort to find original sources, that is, stories that are published by members of the culture of origin. If that is not possible, we can ensure that the original source is identified. In the case of *The Crow's Tale*, for example, Naomi Howarth retells the legend and clearly identifies the story as based on the Lenni Lenape legend. In another example, Canadian Métis story-teller and author David Bouchard collects stories from his own background and often provides a CD with the story in English and in Ojibwe or Cree. When presenting his book *Rainbow Crow*," notes Terry, "I choose not to read or tell the story in my own voice — I use the CD provided so that students can hear Bouchard's voice. I also play the Ojibwe language version or make it available at a literacy listening centre. Bouchard provides comments on the source of his story and on storytelling practices in his culture, such as the use of a circle and sitting as close to Mother Earth as possible.

"Of course, not all published Indigenous stories include oral text in CD form so then I do read the published text aloud and acknowledge the cultural source. This is my preferred way of showing respect."

# Benefits of Engaging in Storytelling

We may choose to weave into the fabric of our classrooms the art of storytelling for its own sake. Stories are entertaining and often offer a welcome respite from activities viewed as work in classroom life. Nonetheless, storytelling should not be considered a frivolous add-on to more serious pursuits. The many social, emotional, and academic benefits associated with storytelling make it well worth exploring.

*Storytelling is good for us.* The ability to spin a good yarn is a key part of being an effective, compelling communicator. Paul J. Zak (2014) uses evidence from neuroscience to back this claim: "When you want to motivate, persuade, or be remembered, start with a story of human struggle and eventual triumph. It will capture people's hearts — by first attracting their brains." And as Pamela Rutledge (2011) puts it, our brains are hardwired to respond to stories:

> Stories are the pathway to engaging our right brain and triggering our imagination. By engaging our imagination, we become participants in the narrative. We can step out of our own shoes, see differently, and increase our empathy for others. Through imagination, we tap into creativity that is the foundation of innovation, self-discovery and change.

These two quotations underscore the positive psychological effects of *listening* to good stories, but they also point to the benefits of *being* a good storyteller. Storytelling ability contributes to effective human communication skills.

*Oral language proficiency is an essential part of being literate.* Storytelling, along with conversation, is one of the fundamental vehicles for oral language learning. Egan (1993, p. 119) writes: "The development of orality is the necessary foundation for the later development of literacy . . . Indeed, a sensitive program of instruction will use the child's oral cultural capacities to make reading and writing engaging and meaningful."

Researchers agree that oral language proficiency is essential in literacy development (see, for example, Cambourne, 2000/2001; and Clay, 2004). Storytelling, in particular, requires listening ability and visualization skills, both key oral language strategies. As this book discusses, talking with children and encouraging talk among children is essential in learning — storytelling stimulates both. The personal nature of the transaction between storyteller and story listener encourages the active co-construction of meaning.

*Story listeners and tellers gain a useful sense of story.* Story listening, along with storytelling and retelling, contributes to the development of a sense of story. When story structures — such as beginning, middle, and end — become internalized, learners are better able to organize their thinking and express themselves with fluency and clarity, using greater sentence variety and a richer vocabulary. The development of *sense of story* has ripple effects for reading comprehension and writing skills (Wells, 2009).

*Retelling and rereading promote improved comprehension and fluency.* The benefits of story listening and storytelling for reading development include improved comprehension, which is related to the abilities to read with fluency and to use mental imagery when reading.

Retelling a story is an effective way of demonstrating comprehension. Technology can be combined with retelling to assess reading comprehension through iPad apps such as Book Creator, where students choose illustrations from texts and use them to retell and discuss a story they have read.

"When one is purely wired for learning through story, the classroom, with all its confusing stimuli, can be an intimidating experience. Storytelling's one-on-one transmission can be miraculous, calming all the jangled nerves and allowing focus. Something literally settles as the mind automatically links into the information being provided. It is both a physical experience and an emotional one."
— Anonymous teacher who has a learning disability

Engaging in storytelling activities such as learning a story to tell by heart involves many *rereadings*. Rereading is a practice long recognized as a fluency builder, its benefits similar to those of Readers theatre (Campbell & Hlusek, 2015; Rasinski, 2006).

*Storytelling fosters engagement in and writing with voice.* An inner sense of story with its effects on organizing thinking, the ability to use a range of sentence types with a wider vocabulary, as well as the capacity to visualize scenes, all contribute to writing skills. This applies to traditional paper-and-pencil or word-processor writing, as well as digital storytelling. When students engage in storytelling or in drama, their engagement in writing improves, and the volume and quality of their writing show significant progress (Campbell & Hlusek, 2009; Parr & Campbell, 2012). The infusion of enticing digital tools into the literacy program contributes to this effect.

Storytelling also contributes to a sense of writer's voice. That is because storytelling involves using one's voice physically, where the teller can gauge the impact on an audience. We saw this effect with Michelle's students after they participated in the activity of telling tales of foolish things they had done (described below).

# Getting Started in Storytelling

How can storytelling activities be embedded throughout everyday classroom life? How can we as teachers make students' own stories more meaningful? How can we delve into the rich traditions of various cultures through discovery of their oral stories? How can we tap into the potential of storytelling for optimizing learning and enhancing the lives of all learners?

As teachers, we can begin by modelling the importance and power of stories through our own storytelling. When we tell anecdotal stories from our own lives, children listen. When we choose our favorite tales from life, from books, or from memory, we share the riches of story, of personal identity, of what it means to be a human being.

We can invite student participation by highlighting personal storytelling through activities such as community sharing circles at the start of each day. Teachers can tell stories. Visiting parents and community members can tell stories. The principal, the custodian, and the school secretary — they all have stories to tell and are potential participants in the daily talk circle. Involving others in storytelling helps to dissolve the walls between the classroom and outside.

## Participation Activities for Introducing Storytelling

Set up brief storytelling activities, such as the four suggested below, to demonstrate that everyone is a storyteller. You might offer a whole-group activity, where everyone tries the same activity, or describe the activities on task cards, where each group uses a different strategy. Before students break into small groups, identify and practise start-and-stop cues so that everyone gets a turn. Encourage students to participate in one or more activities with a partner or in a small group.

**Circle stories:** One person begins a story, and on a signal, the person beside continues the story. Allow students to pass on their turn. Telling a circle story is a great whole-class warm-up. It is also effective in groups of six to eight. Allow a maximum of one minute per teller to keep engagement high. Story starters can be printed on cards and drawn from a box.

**Favorite place stories:** Arrange students in partners or in circles of four or five. Direct them to describe aloud their favorite place, including as much detail as possible so that the listeners can imagine themselves in that place. Ask for volunteers to perform their story for the whole group. Here is a favorite place telling, this one by B.Ed. student Rosemary Scott:

> My favorite place is a rock on the shore of Trout Lake. It has all shades of light and dark greys and silver. When it's wet, you can really see the different greys, and when the sun is shining, the silver glitters. I like to sit there and think.

**Object stories:** Start off this activity by reaching into a bag without looking, picking up an object, thinking about it, and telling a story. This activity can be done in a whole-class circle, or students can meet in smaller story circles, each with a treasure chest or bag of objects to pass around. Objects may include a smooth stone, a feather, and a coin. Each person tells a short tale that the object pulled calls to mind ("This stone reminds me of the time . . ."). Students can tell a familiar tale or a personal story based on the object pulled; they might even tell their story *to* the object, if feeling cautious.

**Name stories:** In preparation, ask students to find out how or why they were given their names or nicknames. Organize students into groups of six, where each person tells a story about his or her name. You may also want to invite parents or grandparents to school to tell stories about how they were named or for whom they were named.

*These four activities are adapted from Parr & Campbell, 2012.*

## Storytelling in a Range of Ways

We can also engage in more formal performance of stories. The stories can be taken from traditional sources such as folktales and from the children's own creations. These include oral texts and retellings of stories, as well as multimodal and digital productions. When storytelling performance becomes part of our literacy instruction, its ripple effects can be amazing! The three traditional pillars of literacy — reading, writing, and oral communication — can all be enhanced in various ways through storytelling.

We begin with informal anecdotal storytelling, since it most closely resembles the kind of storytelling many of us engage in daily. This is followed by two multimodal storytelling activities, one featuring student-created self-portrait storytelling and one using shadow puppets. Finally, we describe the use of traditional tales to explore more formal storytelling.

### Anecdotal Storytelling

Begin by modelling the telling of an anecdote from your past. We recommend telling a tale about a time when you did something foolish. It can be something as simple as locking yourself out of your house or car, or describing an incident from your childhood. Other possible topics for anecdotal stories include the most exciting trip ever experienced, the funniest thing your pet did, or the time you first learned how to do something, such as swim or ride a bike. Topics are drawn from daily life.

Below is an example of a foolish tale that Terry has shared with students in Grades 4 and 5 and teacher candidates. After she finishes, listeners are directed to form groups for telling their own foolish tales. The only instructions are (1) to take turns listening and telling, (2) to tell a true story, and (3) to stick to the posted time limit. One or two minutes each in a group of six works well. This activity is suitable for students in Kindergarten to Grade 8.

---

### The Most Foolish Thing I've Ever Done: Terry

I grew up in a family of six children in Niagara Falls. Two of my brothers, one sister, and I often packed a lunch and embarked on all-day hikes exploring the forests and glens of the gorgeous Niagara landscapes. Our favorite was the Niagara Glen park, set in the escarpment of the lower Niagara River.

On one of these treks, when I was about nine years old, the four of us had made our way down to the rocks at the river's edge. At this point, just below the whirlpool, the mighty Niagara River is compressed into a narrow channel — deep, churning, and dangerous.

My brother dared us to a game of jumping from rock to rock. I followed him from the shoreline rocks over a gap of green river rapids and onto a flat rock partway out into the river. He blithely bounded back, taunting me to follow.

Then I saw where I was.

I froze. I looked at the water and at the small party on shore, and said, "I can't get back!" My legs were trembling. My younger sister started to cry.

It was that sound that spurred me on to gather myself and make the leap.

To this day, if anyone says to me, "Dare ya!" I dig my heels in and refuse to budge.

*(First published in Parr & Campbell, 2012, p. 123)*

---

*[Here I stop and widen my eyes!]*

*[Here I pause for some time and show the audience how my legs were trembling.]*

*[I stand stock-still, not budging.]*

In Michelle's Grade 4–5 class, we used anecdotal storytelling to stimulate storytelling and story writing (see Campbell & Hlusek, 2009, for a full description). At the time, a student teacher was present, so we began by having all three of us tell about a foolish thing we had done. Students then sat in their table groups to share their own stories. After they had told their stories orally, we prompted them to each write a quick draft in their writer's notebook. (The students were using spiral-bound notebooks to record their brainstorming for topics; quick writes; first and subsequent drafts of stories, poems, and nonfiction works; and writing tips.)

Here are samples from recorded student anecdotes:

- I got mad at a hockey game, left the arena in my skates and equipment, and walked home with my skates clattering on the sidewalk. My ankles were killing me by the time I got home. My dad wasn't too happy about having to get my skates sharpened. Again . . .
- I tried to hide my friend's dog under my bed. That didn't go well . . .
- My friends talked me into crawling inside the flip-out sofa in the family room. They had to call my mom to get me out . . .

Over the next three days, students took part in Writers Workshop. They worked on revising, discussing, and editing their stories. Each workshop session ended with an Authors Share time (Michelle's version of Author's Chair). If students did not want to wait until their written work had been published, they could elect to share their works-in-progress and ask for feedback and advice.

Michelle found that allowing daily time for peer feedback seemed to increase student engagement in writing. "The students became more and more articulate about specific elements and strengths of their peers' stories, using phrases such as 'I like the beginning because . . .' or 'I like the words you used when you described . . .,'" she observed. She also noted that when students discussed their stories with one another, they gained help in determining the most effective writing strategies, the best parts of their stories, and the passages they needed to revise. "These discussions seemed to really motivate the kids to keep writing, and to make their writing better."

## Self-Portrait Storytelling

This identity-building experience is a highly creative, unique idea to bring into Grades 2 to 6 classrooms, especially. Because it emphasizes creative individuality, we felt we should use a light touch as far as teacher modelling goes. Michelle often adopts this "minimal modelling" approach, particularly when the students are engaging in creative experiences. She explains:

"As teachers, we sometimes *over-model* what the *end learning goal* of a task should look like. We do this with good intentions. We explicitly model so that success criteria can be met and students can do their best. Through experience, I find that students often replicate the modelled task. The students who want to take a different approach are constantly seeking affirmation and approval: 'Can I do it like this?' 'Is it okay if I change the story characters?' Confidence in their own ideas and creativity is lost, and they are anxious about not succeeding in the assigned task. How does that promote engagement? I found that student voice is lost if we over-model."

For this multimodal storytelling activity, which we call "self-portrait storytelling," we provided large empty wooden frames (normally used for paintings) to emphasize the idea that students were painting self-portraits with their spoken words. From start to finish, from rehearsing orally through to recording using iMovie, the process took four days, using the literacy block of about 100 minutes per day. A possible instructional sequence appears next page.

"I love seeing the look on other people's face when they hear my story. I like getting help from my friends. It helps make the story better."
— Jaimee, Grade 5 student

**To Guide Rather Than to Model**

"I am a collaborator in students' learning. A neat thing that happens is that the students model the possibilities to each other and help each other to hear their 'voice.' A classroom that promotes literacy through hearing student voice enables students to have more autonomy for their learning and more confidence to take risks. That is what an LOL classroom is all about."
— Michelle

*Chris and Sofi smile as they rehearse for their storytelling.*

1. Warm up the class with a read-aloud or an oral story told in the first person. Doing this sets the stage for the first-person tellings students will engage in. We chose *Ooko* by Esmé Shapiro for its direct first-person account of a fox in search of a friend — the fox discovers through experience that it is best to be yourself.

2. Using a frame held in front of the face, the teacher or volunteer guest models a brief personal account. You might talk about how you got a name or nickname, what some of your preferences are, and what wish for the future you have. We kept this very short and emphasized that each person was to determine what to say based on what seemed important: *This is your self-portrait.* This was the right time to implement Michelle's minimal modelling.

3. Ask an overarching question. Michelle gave the students this question to think about: *What is it like to be ME?*

4. Have students break into groups of three to five, seated in circles, with one frame distributed per group. Students talk first about what kinds of facts about themselves they might want to include in an oral self-portrait. When ready, each student takes a turn with the frame and shares a personal story.

5. Students reassemble in the large group, and some volunteer to share their first telling with the class. One student's first telling started like this:

   > Hi. My name is Chris. I love the planets, and I am going to tell you about how I live on this planet called Earth . . .

6. If desired, and weather permitting, take the class outside for photos of students posing with their frames. Michelle's class had a great deal of fun doing this, and their photos were very creative! For instance, when one student told his story about people who are important to him, he invited others into the frame, saying, for example, "Come in here with me, Jay!"

7. On subsequent days, begin with a large-group meeting to recap what has happened so far. Drawing on the initial oral self-portraits and class discussion, Michelle and her students co-created an anchor chart with questions and prompts, reflecting what the students had said about themselves.

8. Have students work in partners. Using an anchor chart like the one below as a guide, they can begin importing photos and recording self-portraits using iMovie.

9. Finally, invite students to present their self-portraits to the whole class. Celebrate!

iMovie is a readily available app provided with Apple products (Macs and iPads). Both of us and our students have found that the steps are quite easy to follow. The key is to begin with a series of good photos.

---

**Self-Portrait Stories: Questions and Prompts**

Overarching question: What is it like to be ME?

*For my iMovie:*
How did I get my name?
What is important about me?
What is it like to walk in my shoes?
What am I going to do to make a difference in the world?
How am I going to leave my mark?

---

Here's what some of Michelle's students thought of self-portrait storytelling:

- "What I liked about telling our stories was getting to know more about the other kids in my class."
- "I found out that there were other kids who were like me in ways I didn't know before. Like we had the same dreams for the future, like helping people and animals by becoming a vet."
- "I liked telling my own story to the class. Lots of kids helped me by asking questions, like, 'If you could go anywhere in the world, where would you go?'"
- "What I liked best about using the frames and making the iMovie was that I made new friends in our class. Both Larry and I want to be construction workers. I didn't know that before!"

## Multimodal Storytelling Using Shadow Puppets

For this activity in Michelle's Grade 3–4 classroom, we combined an oral telling of a story with the use of shadow puppets on an overhead projector. This approach is best applied with a fairly simple folktale with a clear set of characters (animal tales work well). We used *Anansi and the Moss-Covered Rock*, retold by Eric Kimmel, as the basis.

Michelle found an old overhead projector in the school. Low-tech and almost obsolete, overhead projectors make great visual displays possible! Another option is to use shadow puppets behind a sheet.

1. Before the storytelling activity, make the essential shadow puppets, either by yourself or with a group of students. Using the characters in the story (Anansi the spider, a lion, an elephant, and Little Bush Deer, as well as a few other animals), we made cut-out shapes using card stock and attached craft sticks to manipulate. We made the puppets small enough to fit easily onto an overhead projector.
2. Learn the story to tell orally, or assign a narrator while you manipulate the puppets. Don't memorize so much as find the pattern in the tale. Use the animals to remind you of the order of events. Rehearse!
3. Introduce the story. Terry spoke briefly about the trickster character Anansi the spider, the African origin of the Anansi stories, and the popularity of the tales in the West Indies, particularly in Jamaica.
4. Tell the story and show the puppets moving around, using the overhead projector.
5. Allow some time for large-group oral response, and discuss what the students would like to do. Michelle told them they might retell the story they had just heard, taking turns to use the puppets and the projector; tell their own version of the story; or create a new story entirely.
6. *Examples of what the students did:* After a brief discussion, students quickly decided what they wanted to do.
   - One group of three chose to use the existing puppets to tell a new story.
   - A group of six gathered around Dana, who had immediately said, "We can make our own shadow puppets!" Members proceeded to create a new story based on the idea of a magic object. One student wrote the story as they discussed it while the others began drawing and cutting out animal characters along with a bolt of lightning that had magical powers. As they worked, they continually tested the visual appearance of their cut-outs, using the projector.
   - Two students talked about the magic of the eagle feather. One told about finding an eagle feather when walking in the bush with his family. The

other recounted seeing an eagle on Manitoulin Island. They decided to compose a story about "the eagle who lost a feather" using just two cutouts, one of an eagle, the other of a single feather.

- One student worked solo, creating puppets of a magic tree and three human characters.

By the end of that first literacy block, two groups had presented their stories using the overhead projector. The others were given more time on the next day and presented to a group whose members had been away at a choir festival.

## Storytelling Performance

**Teaching Considerations**

*What texts might be suitable for your group?*
Before teaching students how to be storytellers, consider age, reading levels, interests, cultural backgrounds, and what sorts of stories sound well when spoken aloud.

*How will you group children?*
Partners work well for telling stories, but small groups can be successful as well.

*How much time and space will you need for rehearsal and for final performance?*

*How will you assess both process and performance?*
For ideas, please see "Storytelling Assessment Checklist" on page 102.

Some stories seem designed for oral performance. They are familiar-sounding and flow easily when read aloud. Traditional stories, such as folktales, fables, and legends, tend to exemplify this quality because they come from oral sources.

Traditional tales also allow the teller to word the stories in a way that will facilitate oral telling (when vocabulary is unfamiliar or difficult to pronounce, for example). When our students are reading, discussing, rewriting, and retelling stories, we want them to think deeply about the story meaning as they process print texts into oral speech. Their understanding of the story should be evident in the fluent and expressive way they tell or retell the tale. In this way, comprehension and fluency are integrally linked with oral expression. The choice of text is central.

For this activity, we chose Arnold Lobel's *Fables*, a collection of one-page stories. For an initial foray into oral storytelling, the one-page fables are a perfect length. We read the stories aloud before introducing them to the students to ensure that they had the flow essential for oral telling. The reading level (about Grades 2 to 4) was within the range of most students in the class, and extra support was provided when needed; for example, a partner would read aloud a story to a peer who was less comfortable. Students formed partners or small groups and together chose a story they liked and wished to present. In that way, students exercised choice as well.

We began with modelling the telling of a short familiar tale. Two good examples are "The Three Billy Goats Gruff" and "The Three Little Pigs." In this instance, Terry modelled how to tell a story orally by using an interactive text, "I'm Tipingee, She's Tipingee, We're Tipingee, Too" from Diane Wolkstein's *The Magic Orange Tree: And Other Haitian Folktales*. Students joined in on the repeated refrain, which is the same as the story's title. Terry then posted on chart paper a series of steps to help tellers learn a story "by heart."

These steps are recommendations only. It is not necessary to follow every step. For example, creating a storyboard may be unnecessary for some learners, but helpful for strongly visual learners.

## Terry's 10 Steps for Storytellers

1. Choose a story you really like. Read several stories to find the right one.
2. Read the chosen story silently two or three times, picturing the story in your mind as you read.
3. Read the story aloud to your partner or other members of your small group.
4. Visualize all the details of the story, and discuss them.
5. Within your group, create a storyboard, using at least three cartoon box frames, to show the main events of the story with pictures and captions.
6. Tell the story to your partner using the storyboard. Don't worry about using the exact words from the book.
7. Tell the story again without the storyboard. Visualize as you tell.
8. Reread the story to check for missing parts or special words you want to remember.
9. Practise! Practise! Practise!
10. Trust the story and yourself. Tell it to your story circle.

*(Adapted from Parr & Campbell, 2012, p. 127)*

*Instructional Sequence*

The following outlines what Michelle's students did over a one-week period during the literacy block:

1. We discussed how to learn a story using "Terry's 10 Steps for Storytellers," above.
2. Copies of Lobel's one-page fables were distributed to partners or groups.
3. Daily time was provided to read and discuss the stories. Together, students chose the story they wanted to present. Two students decided to tell their tales individually, while groups of two, three, and up to four students presented their stories together. Each group told one story. Some groups had a narrator with participants who acted, recited, or read their lines, and some sang and danced their parts.
4. Students were encouraged to get inside the story. Michelle provided plenty of time for collaborative talk to make sense of the stories, make personal connections, figure out unfamiliar vocabulary, and rewrite the text to feel comfortable with the wording if necessary. Independently, most students discussed the context of the story to figure out vocabulary that was new to them. Several rewrote some lines that they considered old-fashioned to make them sound and feel more natural when said aloud. For example, "I'm so very busy" became "I'm busy."
5. Students rehearsed their stories (reading from scripts) with their own partner or small group. The two solo storytellers practised together. Some groups chose to use props and costume pieces, all collected from the classroom recycling centre.
6. Students then rehearsed with another pair or small group, listening and providing feedback. We circulated and provided tips as needed on eye contact and vocal effects, such as volume, pitch, and pacing. (See "Storytelling

Assessment Checklist" on page 102.) Students were encouraged to tell by heart rather than to memorize, using their own words as much as possible. During rehearsals, some students progressed to telling the story by heart, while others kept their scripts in hand, apparently just for security — "in case I go blank" said one — since they rarely referred to them.

7. In consultation with the students, we established a day and time for the performances. We kept this flexible because the students took varying lengths of time to feel ready to present.

*Students Taking Ownership of Performance*

- Students set up the stage, managed props and costumes, and referred to scripts if needed. They decided to use a semi-circle, with their stage at the open end, allowing everyone to hear and view.
- The students decided on the program order. When an individual or small group was ready, they went onstage.
- The performances were followed by student-led feedback.
- Students indicated that they were aware of areas they might improve upon. After discussing the event together, they suggested that the class prepare another storytelling session.

*An account of this experience was first published in* The Reading Teacher *in 2015.*

Michelle's Grade 3 students accomplished these performances in one week. They read some challenging material and made it their own through rehearsal and performance. They used movement, song, visual art, and objects to enhance their presentations. They cooperated in pairs and in small groups to achieve success *in a variety of ways* — there was no single right way to do this. Even those who performed solo acts were supported by peers during rehearsals.

---

## Tales for Telling and Retelling

*Kindergarten to Grade 3*

*The Three Billy Goats Gruff*, retold by P. C. Asbjornsen and J. E. Moe, illustrated by Marcia Brown

*The Three Little Pigs*, retold by Annette Smith, illustrated by Isabel Lowe

*Too Much Talk: A West African Folktale*, retold by Angela Shelf Medearis

*Grades 3 to 5*

*Anansi and the Moss-Covered Rock*, adapted by Eric A. Kimmel, illustrated by Janet Stevens

*The Legend of the Lady Slipper*, adapted by Margi Preus and Lise Lunge-Larsen, illustrated by Andrea Arroyo

*Why Mosquitoes Buzz in People's Ears*, by Verna Aardema, illustrated by Diane and Leo Dillon

*Grades 4 to 6*

*Eric Carle's Treasury of Classic Stories for Children*

*How the Robin Got Its Red Breast: A Legend of the Sechelt People*, by the Sechelt Nation, illustrated by Charlie Craigan

*The Magic Orange Tree: And Other Haitian Folktales*, collected by Diane Wolkstein

---

*Grades 5 to 8*
*Favorite Folktales from Around the World*, edited by Jane Yolen
*Out of Everywhere, New Tales for Canada* by Jan Andrews, illustrated by
  Simon Ng

## Fire from the Spoken Word

The art of storytelling involves our hearts and minds in ways that deeply connect us as teachers and learners. Storytelling is a powerful oral communication skill to pass on to the new generation of students. Considering its many benefits, from the academic to the emotional, it is worth infusing into our classroom life as part of our dynamic everyday speaking and listening activities.

Last word goes to Ruth Sawyer, the great storyteller and author of *The Way of the Storyteller*:

> To be a good storyteller one must be gloriously alive. It is not possible
> to kindle fresh fires from burned-out embers. I have noticed that the
> best of the traditional storytellers whom I have heard have been those
> who live close to the heart of things — to the earth, the sea, wind and
> weather. They have been those who knew solitude, silence. They have
> been given unbroken time in which to feel deeply, to reach constantly for
> understanding. They have come to know the power of the spoken word.
> (Sawyer, 1942/1970, p. 28)

# Storytelling Assessment Checklist

Name: _____  Date: _____

*Criteria*                                      *Comments*

**Listens** attentively to stories

**Responds** to stories (e.g., through discussion, art, and drama)

**Shares** personal anecdotes and stories

**Tells** oral stories
- ☐ with a partner
- ☐ in a small group
- ☐ in a large group

**Retells** stories, maintaining
- ☐ plot and story problem
- ☐ main characters
- ☐ setting
- ☐ vocabulary

**Performs** oral stories, demonstrating
- ☐ use of vocal effects, including tone, pace, pitch, and volume
- ☐ fluent, expressive speech
- ☐ eye contact with audience
- ☐ facial expression

Notes:

Pembroke Publishers ©2017 *Literacy Out Loud* by Terry Anne Campbell and Michelle E. McMartin ISBN 978-1-55138-323-1

# 8

# Using Talk Circles for Readers Theatre

*Knowing the connection between time spent reading and academic progress, I strive in my career to find ways to "turn on" students to reading. In my years as an elementary and middle school teacher, a professor of reading methods in a teacher preparation program, and the mother of a resistant reader, the single most motivating activity I have ever found is Readers Theater.*

*— Jo Worthy, 2005, p. 9*

*Readers Theatre has been a routine part of my classroom literacy program for a long time. Using talk circles for rehearsing and providing feedback has bumped up performance levels to new heights.*

*— Lorna MacKenzie, Grade 5 teacher*

Readers theatre is implemented in many classrooms because it is a highly motivating oral activity, especially for reluctant readers and nervous speakers. It can also offer opportunities for high achievers or gifted students to develop skills in collaboration and leadership in mixed-ability groupings. It is a simple and low-risk way to foster enjoyment in reading aloud together.

This chapter describes ways of creating effective Readers theatre groups using talk circles. There, the benefits reside in the collaborative discussions and rehearsals, which are optimized by the circle formation. We describe how to gradually increase performance levels by *expanding the circles* — that is, by having the members of one circle join another circle to rehearse performances and provide and receive feedback. Talk circles provide a more intensive rehearsal experience than would happen when individual groups rehearse in isolation or with only teacher feedback. Students are motivated to polish their performances because they receive useful feedback from their peers. The performance levels are noticeably higher when rehearsal time allows in-depth feedback for improving.

# What Readers Theatre Does

As drama through oral expression, Readers theatre involves small groups of students reading prepared scripts and performing with purpose, using primarily their voices to convey the meaning of text. Eventually, students can be engaged in creating their own scripts. The many benefits of Readers theatre include collaborative group work, literary appreciation, greater confidence in oral language ability, increased vocabulary through repetition, and especially, reading fluency.

Garrett and O'Connor (2010) summarize Readers theatre as "an instructional method that connects quality literature, oral reading, drama, and several research-based practices" (p. 7). Unlike conventional dramatic performances, this strategy is based on oral reading of rehearsed scripts. No memorization is required. Props and costumes are optional. The focus is on expressive reading using one's voice. Readers theatre provides students with real purpose for rereading texts as they rehearse for performance.

## A Way to Improve Reading Fluency

Repeated reading is a well-known strategy for improving reading fluency. The problem is that without a purpose, repeated readings of the same text can become a tedious chore. However, once the goal is to *perform* the text in some way, rereadings become driven by a definite purpose.

In the case of Readers theatre, the purpose of rereading a text is to practise for the *performance* of a dramatic read-aloud to an audience. Teachers who have implemented Readers theatre have observed how reading fluency improves (Worthy & Prater, 2002). Indeed, many educators and researchers have observed and written about this power of Readers theatre to improve reading fluency (e.g., Jackson, Jenkins, & January-Vance, 2014; Rasinski, 2006). Rasinski observes:

> What would really inspire me to engage in repeated reading or rehearsal
> is performance. If I were to give an oral reading performance of a passage,
> I would most certainly have an incentive to practice, rehearse, or engage
> in repeated readings. All of us, at one time or another, have read orally
> for an audience. It is likely that we practiced in advance of that reading,
> and if we didn't it is likely that we wish we had. To continue with this line
> of reasoning, if performance is the incentive to practice, then we need to
> ask what kinds of texts lend themselves to expressive oral performance . . .
> (2006, p. 305)

The kinds of texts used in Readers theatre include stories with clear characters and short lines of dialogue. Readers theatre can also use interactive poetry, chants, and rhymes, much like choral speaking (see Chapter 6). It calls for texts that can be easily read aloud with expression and understanding. Rasinski concludes, "To me these texts are the perfect fit for fluency instruction and repeated readings" (2006, p. 305).

## Fostering Listening and Audience Awareness

In addition to promoting oral expression, taking part in Readers theatre offers students a prime opportunity to work on *listening skills*. During rehearsals and performances, readers must listen carefully to know when to come in with their own lines. The use of *expanding circles* ensures that the responses of the listeners become a focus just as the presentations by the readers are. The audience members play a role in learning how to appreciate a performance and how to provide constructive critique.

## Getting Started with Readers Theatre

The ideas outlined below are suitable for students in Grades 1 to 8 but can be adapted for Kindergarten students. Information specific to Kindergarten students follows.

As this list suggests, performance requirements are quite modest. You will need

- one director, likely yourself but it could be another individual interested in providing a meaningful oral language experience for children
- students (as many as you have)
- a script, which can be produced by others or created by the students
- chairs arranged in a circle or at a circular table for organizing and rehearsing
- stools, chairs, or benches for performing for an audience (The script may provide guidance.)
- folders, preferably black, one for each script needed

To prepare, select a script, or work with students to produce one. To produce a script with students, choose a text with plenty of dialogue, and make a copy for each group member. Read aloud the lines said by each character, have the students repeat them, and show students how to highlight just the words spoken aloud. If desired, assign a narrator for the parts remaining. This process might be modelled on an interactive whiteboard first, so that the whole class gets the idea. Books such as the Stella series by Marie-Louise Gay can be used with students as young as Grade 2 to create Readers theatre scripts because they are written entirely in dialogue. It may take some extra time, but typing out the final script and making photocopies is worth the effort, as it will help the students rehearse independently later.

Based on stories in the public domain, teacher-adapted scripts can be created. Again, choose stories with plenty of dialogue. For a sample teacher-adapted script, see pages 113 and 114.

Separate students into two groups: the readers and those who will later form the audience. Many teachers use the model of working with guided reading groups. While you work with one group, the other students are busy reading silently or working quietly in their small groups. You can either assign roles to readers or have students make the decisions. Help students learn their parts as readers, keeping in mind that the focus is on oral interpretation. You or the readers may decide that a few props are appropriate.

Set up the "stage" in a way that suits the script. For example, for a performance of Shel Silverstein's poem "Sick," readers sat in a row behind each other and leaned out to left or right on their turn. Ensure that scripts are placed in black folders and that the readers' faces can be clearly seen so that their voices project well. Doing so makes the performance look and sound professional.

Help listeners identify their role and tasks. As the script is presented, audience members can play the roles of listeners and critics, prepared to make suggestions later for the improvement of the performance.

Once the performance is over, hold a large-group discussion with the audience and readers to evaluate the presentation. Be sure to remind both performers and audience that the feedback should be offered and received in the spirit of encouraging improvements. Later, help the small group of performers assess how well members collaborated with an aim to improving cooperation and collaborative problem-solving. (See "Success Criteria for Readers Theatre" on page 110.)

### Adapting Readers Theatre for Kindergarten

Kindergartners or students with limited reading ability can participate in Readers theatre with a few key adaptations. First, print their parts on numbered and color-coded cards, and coach them individually and as a group. You or an older, confident reader can serve as the narrator and signal when each reader should come in.

Whitney Underhill, a teacher candidate, did this successfully with a group of Kindergarten students. She used color-coded cards and rehearsed cues for the young readers:

"I wrote a script called 'Forest Adventure' for five characters: two rabbits, an owl, a mouse, and a frog. Each character had their short lines printed on color-coded cards in numbered order. Each card also had images of their character to cue them. One of the adults (me, Whitney, and later the teacher and the early childhood educator for the next groups) read the narrated parts with some stage directions. Each of their lines was very short, for example, 'I'm lost!' and 'Do you know where my home is?'

"With practice, the first group performed beautifully, and the rest of the class formed groups to try it out so that everyone had a turn."

## Demonstration of Readers Theatre with Critical Listeners

Michelle wanted to try using talk circles to improve the performance level of her Grade 3–4 students in Readers theatre. So, we decided to try a large-group version of Readers theatre in an all-inclusive circle to introduce the idea of the audience providing helpful feedback. We both read in role, about half the students were scattered throughout the circle as readers, and the rest of the students were designated as the audience. We told the audience members that their role was to help us improve our performance.

We adapted Jon Klassen's *I Want My Hat Back*, with Michelle as Bear, Terry as Rabbit, a student as narrator, and several students as Fox, Frog, Turtle, Snake, Possum, and Deer. Each animal had his or her lines on a card, and the narrator cued which animal would come in next. The only prop we used was a red cap. It was worn by Rabbit, who had taken it from Bear — Terry did this in role right before the performance.

In this instance, we did not rehearse first because we wanted the audience of listeners to provide feedback on our first attempt, hoping that they would see how important practice is when preparing Readers theatre. The student participants were given their cue cards about 15 minutes ahead of time so that they could become familiar with their lines.

## Audience Feedback: Practise!

The students spontaneously made predictions about the significance of the hat, laughing and saying, "Mrs. McMartin looks like a gangster" [Michelle had the ball cap on sideways], and when Terry took the hat, they laughed and said, "You can't just take her hat!"

We went right through the script, and some of the students projected the character of their animal using their voice. For example, Bear asks Snake, "Have you seen my hat?" Snake answers, "I sssaw a hat once-ssss. It wasss blue and round." When it came to Possum, however, it was different. Bear asked, as usual, "Have you seen my hat?" Possum was expected to say, "No, I have not seen your hat" but instead asked, "What's a hat?" As an aside, the boy reading Possum's lines said, "I don't know what a Possum is, but it must be really stupid."

Once we finished the performance, we asked the audience members what they thought about it and how we might improve it. Here is a sampling of their comments:

- "It was very funny. It should have been longer, with more animals, and it would have been even funnier."
- "Some of you should have read with more expression, and try to sound like the animal. Like the frog: you should croak or sound croaky."
- "Mrs. Campbell, you were funny, but you didn't sound like a Rabbit."
- "There should be some actions so we would know what the animal is. Like, the turtle could move like this . . ." [The student got up and demonstrated a slow-moving turtle.]
- "Or . . . the turtle could just talk really slow. Not fast, like the Rabbit."
- "The animals need to say their lines right away, not waiting, like."

When we asked them how we might get the performance to be more like what they wanted, they all agreed on the way: we must *practise*.

## Readers Theatre in Small Groups

After summing up this large-group experience, we followed up with small-group Readers theatre. We had several scripts to choose from and presented the titles and basic ideas for each script. Students chose the scripts they were drawn to and formed groups accordingly. Michelle asked them what doing their personal best in Readers theatre meant. They all said, "Practise!"

Students had the next 20 minutes to rehearse, and then they could perform and receive feedback, and then rehearse again to improve.

Children of this age seem best able to identify with and understand individual characters through the help of costume and set pieces. See Michelle's "Observations and Reflections," next page.

Most groups were composed of members of mixed reading and oral language levels. In all cases, more confident readers and speakers offered support by sitting beside less confident ones and quietly prompting and whispering their lines to them as needed.

The groups read through their scripts, highlighted their parts, and rehearsed in circles. Although the students were told that for Readers theatre they had only to read their lines, as we had modelled, most of them *immediately and spontaneously* began creating small sets using classroom furniture and costume pieces, such as paper ears for animals. They rehearsed once more with their impromptu props.

Over the next three days, the cycle of rehearsal and feedback from peers in small groups continued. By the end of the week, each group had received suggestions from at least one other group and had had time to implement changes. They were all ready for final performances by each group in front of the whole class. They all participated, enjoyed the process, and seemed happy with their performances.

During a final large-group circle held to self-assess, students recognized that receiving suggestions from their classmates in small groups during the rehearsal process had helped them to improve. *And they still saw ways to improve further.* Some of those who were reluctant at first were begging to "do this again"!

---

### Observations and Reflections: Michelle

I've noticed that for this age group, particularly with the Grade 3 students, their natural inclination is to focus on the *theatre* aspect of Readers theatre. As soon as the groups are formed and scripts are chosen, they want to create props, costumes, and sets. The students will focus on vocal expression when working on Readers theatre in the whole group where there is teacher guidance. However, when they move to independent practice, they invariably turn the experience into a *play*. This has happened with every Grade 3 class I've taught — all five of them! On the other hand, when I taught a Grade 4–5 class, students could understand the concept of how to use mainly your voice and oral expression to convey a character.

The Grade 3 students seem to take performance more holistically, and concretely, in a way. For them, it's about movement, costumes, *becoming the character*, not just reading the lines. I've never stopped them, because this involves their creative impetus at work. Besides, if this experience is to get students *collaborating*, *using oral expression*, and *rereading for fluency*, we are still achieving those ends.

---

## Ten Steps to Successful Readers Theatre

Mixed-ability groups work well.

1. Choose texts. Criteria include aiming for moderate reading challenge, with the provision of supports for those who require it; texts of one or two pages, which will yield a performance of two to five minutes; and roles for two to eight readers. The text should include lines of dialogue or lend itself to being easily converted to dialogue. It can be a dramatic or humorous story, or a nonfiction piece suitable for dialogue.

   As for sources for scripts, consider specially produced scripts, such as those in *Readers Theater for Building Fluency: Strategies and Scripts for Making the Most of This Highly Effective, Motivating, and Research-Based Approach to Oral Reading*, by Jo Worthy. You might also choose short tales in anthologies or picture book texts with roles for narrator(s) and two to six individual characters. *Fables* by Arnold Lobel is an example. There are also public domain stories and free scripts online, for example, Aaron Shepard's RT Page: Scripts and Tips for Reader's Theater, a great source for free scripts and templates for creating scripts (www.aaronshep.com/rt). Finally, it is possible to draw on students' own stories and scripts created for Readers theatre.

2. Form groups. Groups can consist of two to eight readers, with there being mixed ability in reading and speaking. Match the readers with the scripts, providing some choice, if possible.

3. Organize time and resources.
   - Allow about one week from first reading to final performance with daily time for rehearsal during your literacy block.

- Provide copies of the script for each reader, in folders. Have a place for students to store their folders where they can easily retrieve them for practice (alone or in their group).
- Arrange for the use of a circular table or chairs in a circle and provide clipboards if needed.
- Provide light-colored highlighters and sticky notes for ongoing notes to themselves about volume, tempo, changes to the lines, and so on.

4. Hold a first reading, providing guidance, facilitating talk, and assigning roles. Depending on grade and reading level, you may want to read the entire script aloud first as students follow along in their copies. Allow time for them to read through the script together, not choosing roles yet.

   Allow time for students to talk about the story, the characters involved, and what they are showing about themselves through their speech. Possible prompts: What kind of character is A? How do you think she might sound? How would B sound? Loud and confident, or quiet and shy? Are there parts in this where you might want to say the lines all together?

   In collaboration with group members, students now choose roles. Typically, there are one or two narrators and two or three characters. Some teacher guidance is usually required the first time that students encounter Readers theatre.

   Once they know their roles, show them how to highlight their lines. Sometimes, highlighting requires careful guidance, even with older (junior age) students.

5. Rehearse readings on subsequent days. Supervise and guide as needed, focusing on oral expression. Provide ongoing feedback and invite students to make their own reflections frequently. Allow more and more time for independent practice.

6. When two circles are ready — when the members of two circles can read their lines in sequence fairly smoothly — direct the two circles to join into one large circle. That will allow each group to present to the other. Encourage constructive critique, focusing on specific ways they can improve their oral expression. For example, "Crow, can you make your voice croakier?" or "Mouse, can you change the pitch to higher, but not too quiet?"

7. Keep creating expanded circles until all have had a turn rehearsing with another circle.

8. Provide time for group talk to discuss how students will use feedback, and provide one more rehearsal time for each group back in their original circle formation.

9. Decide on a performance day or days. Times may be staggered to accommodate groups that are ready at different times.

10. When it's time to perform, review the roles of the readers and of the audience (see the success criteria that follow), and begin performing!

> ### Success Criteria for Readers Theatre
>
> As a reader:
>
> I participated in my circle's discussions.
>
> I helped to make decisions about choosing roles fairly.
>
> I came to rehearsals with my script ready.
>
> I listened and made notes about how to read my part based on feedback from my circle and the expanded circle.
>
> I stayed focused by listening to the other readers in my circle and following my script.
>
> I always worked towards my personal best during rehearsals and performance.
>
> As an audience member:
>
> I listened attentively to rehearsals and performances.
>
> I showed appreciation by giving positive feedback.
>
> I offered suggestions for making performances better.

## Co-creating Scripts

Depending on their age and familiarity with Readers theatre, students can co-create scripts. If in Grades 2 to 4, they can work with a teacher to adapt a story text into a script. If in Grades 4 to 8, they can create a Readers theatre script in a small group either with teacher guidance or with little or no support needed from the teacher.

### Student-Adapted Scripts

Show students how to take texts and transform them into scripts. Select one- to two-page stories, and give them copies to mark up using highlighters and sticky notes. This process works well as partner work or with small groups of three or four. Here is a sample sequence which was used with Grade 4 students:

- Select a one-page fable from the Lobel collection and give each of the partners or small group members a copy.
- Guide students to read the story aloud together. For some students, you may need to read the story aloud to them first as they follow along.
- Together, talk about the story as you would after a read-aloud.
- Direct students to notice the characters and what they are saying.
- Taking one character at a time, ask a student to say aloud what the character says. Highlight just those words (not tags, such as "he said").
- Continue with other characters' speeches, using different colored highlighters. The non-highlighted parts will be for the narrator. Use sticky notes to change any lines as desired for flow.
- Make a clean version and distribute copies. Discuss with the students who will play what role. Invite them to get into rehearsal and prepare a performance.

## Student-Composed Scripts

Students who are experienced in Readers theatre and are fluent readers and writers (approximately Grades 4 to 8) are probably ready to compose their own scripts "from scratch." They will, however, benefit from some guidance, as this example provided by a B.Ed. student indicates.

Stefan Saad, a teacher candidate in a Grade 5 placement, worked with a group of six students who decided to prepare their own script for presenting as Readers theatre. Here are some of his observations:

"The group I was working with had prior experience doing Readers theatre using prepared scripts. Some remembered being in groups who had a few squabbles over parts — who had the best and biggest parts, and so on.

"After listing several ideas for scripts, they came to a consensus on a story line: It would be about two detectives tracking down a thief who had stolen a famous painting (they had recently read the mystery novel, *Chasing Vermeer*, by Blue Valliett, but their own story would be 'different'). The characters would be two detectives (a boy and a girl), a gallery attendant, and two witnesses. The sixth person would be narrator.

"When they began discussing how they would write the script and choose roles fairly, they decided they would *count the number of words each reader got*, so that everyone had an equal part. It took them two days to write the script, with many revisions, but they managed! I photocopied the final script so everyone had a copy. They rehearsed during the following two days and were ready by Friday. They were so pleased with themselves, and they did a fabulous job. All in one week!"

## Independent Readers Theatre Circles

Once students are familiar with the Readers theatre process — that is, they have read and rehearsed prepared scripts in their own circles and in one or more expanded circles, and have performed their work — they may be ready for independent work. In a Readers theatre circle at a literacy centre, students could co-create their own scripts. These scripts might be adapted from an existing story or composed from scratch. The centre could follow guidelines like these, which the teacher would review with students before they begin to work independently:

1. Brainstorm ideas for scripts and make a decision.
2. Reread your selected text carefully, highlighting or noting lines you'd like to use or adapt in your script.
3. Determine how many characters and narrators you need.
4. Create a script, with all members participating. Make sure that everyone has a set of colored cue cards or sticky notes so that you can each write your lines down and then rearrange until your ideal script is found.
5. Revise, edit, and polish your script; ensure that everyone has a copy.
6. Rehearse your script, paying attention to how your voices are used to bring characters to life and show how they feel, who they are, or how they fit in with the story. When rehearsing, focus on developing fluency, pace, volume, and expression.

*(Parr & Campbell, 2012, p. 112)*

On pages 113 and 114, you will find "Readers Theatre: The Talkative Tortoise," based on a traditional folktale. This script was adapted by Terry and would work especially well in Grades 4 to 6. It requires seven readers (note the overlapping roles) and takes about five minutes to perform.

## Suggested Resources for Readers Theatre

- *Kindergarten to Grade 2:* For four or five readers: "The Three Little Pigs," "Goldilocks and the Three Bears," "The Three Billy Goats Gruff," or other simple folktales (Adapt any picture-book version, for example, Paul Galdone's retellings.)
- *Grades 1 to 2:* For four to six readers: *Madeline* by Ludwig Bemelmans (Adapt for two to four narrators, Madeline, Miss Clavel, and everyone for the girls.)
- *Grades 2 to 3:* For two readers: *Stella, Queen of the Snow* by Marie-Louise Gay (There is no need to adapt; text is written in two voices only.)
  For four to six readers: *I Want My Hat Back* by Jon Klassen (Written in dialogue, this text is easily adapted.)
- *Grades 3 to 5:* For four readers: "The Zax" by Dr. Seuss, in *The Sneetches and Other Stories* (for North-going Zax, South-going Zax, and two narrators); *My Lucky Day* by Keiko Kasza (for Piglet, Mr. Fox, and two narrators)
  For four to six readers: *Fables* by Arnold Lobel (adaptable short tales)
- *Grades 4 to 8:* For four to six readers: *The True Story of the Three Little Pigs* by Jon Scieszka; *The Stinky Cheese Man and Other Fairly Stupid Tales* by Jon Scieszka; anthologies of folk and fairy tales found in the public domain, for example, *English Fairy Tales*, collected by Joseph Jacobs; and *Canadian Wonder Tales*, collected by Cyrus MacMillan (available in the International Folktale Collection database)

# Readers Theatre: The Talkative Tortoise

*Characters*

N1   Narrator 1           T     Tortoise
N2   Narrator 2           K     King
D1   Wild Duck 1          KA    King's Adviser
D2   Wild Duck 2

*N1:* Long ago, a very clever girl was brought up in the King's palace.

*N2:* When she grew up, she was so smart and knew so much she was made the King's Adviser. She gave the King good advice.

*N1:* But there was a problem with this King. Although he was a kind man, he never stopped talking.

*N2:* Once he started speaking, no one else could get in a single word!

*N1:* Now the Adviser saw this. She knew that he would be a better King if he could be cured of his talkativeness.

*N2:* She constantly looked for ways of doing this.

*N1:* Now, at that time, there happened to be a tortoise living in a pond outside the palace grounds.

*N2:* This tortoise had the same problem as the king: it could not stop talking!

*N1:* The tortoise had become friends with two wild ducks. One day, the ducks said:

*D1 and D2 together:*
    Friend tortoise! The place where we live, at the Golden Cave on Mount Beautiful, is a delightful spot. Will you come there with us?

*T:* Yes! But how can I get there?

*D1 and D2 together:*
    We can take you, if you can only hold your tongue and will say nothing to anybody. You must not talk!

*T:* Oh! That I can do! Take me with you!

*D1 and D2 together:*
    Good! Tortoise, bite down hard on this stick. We will take the two ends in our beaks and fly up into the air carrying you with us. Remember not to talk!

*N1 and N2:* And the ducks flew up in the air carrying the tortoise between them!

Pembroke Publishers ©2017 *Literacy Out Loud* by Terry Anne Campbell and Michelle E. McMartin ISBN 978-1-55138-323-1

*N1:* The villagers saw the wild ducks carrying the tortoise. They yelled:

*N1, N2, D1, D2 together as villagers:*
**Look! Two wild ducks are carrying a tortoise along on a stick!**

*N2:* Now, the tortoise just had to say something back to the villagers.

*N1:* He yelled back:

*T:* If my friends choose to carry me, what is that to you?

*N2:* The two ducks were flying over the King's palace just as Tortoise spoke.

*N1:* And Tortoise let go of the stick in order to talk.

*N2:* And down went Tortoise. Right in the middle of the courtyard!

*N1, N2, D1, and D2 as villagers:*
**A tortoise has fallen in the open courtyard and has split in two!**

*N1:* The King went to the place where Tortoise fell and brought his Adviser and his servants.

*K:* Adviser! Teacher! How has this Tortoise fallen here?

*KA (talking to the audience, not speaking yet to the King):*
I have waited so long for something to happen so that the King would be cured of his talkativeness. This tortoise must have made friends with the wild ducks; and they must have made him bite hold of the stick, and have flown up into the air to take him to the hills. But the tortoise was not able to keep his mouth closed. When he hears anyone else talk, he must say something. And he let go of the stick. And so he fell down from the sky and lost his life.

*To the King, KA says:*
Truly, O king! Those who are called chatter-boxes — people who cannot stop talking — come to grief like this! By talking too much, this tortoise fell to his end! O King, speak wise words, but do not talk all the time!

*K:* Teacher, Adviser! Are you speaking about me?

*KA:* O great King! I am talking to you, and to all who talk too much without thinking. Talk after your thinking is clear, or you may end up like poor Tortoise here.

*All:* **From that day on, the King held back from so much talking. He became a man of few words and a much wiser king.**

Adapted by Terry Campbell from "The Talkative Tortoise," in *Indian Fairy Tales*, selected and edited by Joseph Jacobs (London/New York, 1912; public domain, 2013).

Pembroke Publishers ©2017 *Literacy Out Loud* by Terry Anne Campbell and Michelle E. McMartin ISBN 978-1-55138-323-1

114

# 9

## Coming Full Circle

*If people stand in a circle long enough, they'll eventually begin to dance.*

— *George Carlin*

*Talking makes a different kind of experience in class. Learning is fun, and it seems easier too.*

— *Sadi, Grade 4 student*

In this final chapter of *Literacy Out Loud*, we come full circle. We began by presenting our beliefs, feelings, ideas, and background research about why classroom talk matters: why Literacy should be expressed and experienced Out Loud in the classroom. We shared some strategies and activities as well as some experiences with Michelle's students trying out those strategies and activities. As George Carlin observes, stand in a circle long enough, and you're bound to begin to dance. We began with the community talk circle, and we saw how that led to participation in a series of dance-like moves, from talking, to reading good books together, to drawing and talking some more, to reciting and composing poetry, to performing drama, storytelling, and Readers theatre, all with more talk along the way. Since Michelle's classroom was the stage, and her students the actors as speakers and listeners, the last words are from Michelle and her students.

### The Beauty of the Circle

"Leo Buscaglia was my inspiration to becoming a teacher," Michelle affirms. "He wrote, 'Too often we underestimate the power of a touch, a smile, a kind word, a listening ear, an honest compliment or the smallest act of caring, all which have the potential to turn a life around.' That is the beauty of the circle, the LOL classroom, the talk community.

"It is my responsibility as a teacher to prepare my students to be active participants in 21st-century literacies. A 21st-century learner needs to be a problem solver, collaborator, and critical thinker. A 21st-century learner also needs to be technologically literate and self-confident. As we have described in this book, a dialogic, or talk, classroom can address all of these characteristic identities."

---

### Talk in the Classroom: Seven Kinds of Reasons

Robin Alexander (2017) writes about the value of dialogic teaching. He sums up solid reasons for a talk classroom: reasons that reinforce the ones we spoke about throughout the book.

1. *Communicative:* Talk is humankind's principal means of communication.
2. *Social:* Talk builds relationships, confidence, and sense of self.
3. *Cultural:* Talk creates and sustains individual and collective identities.
4. *Neuroscientific:* Language, especially spoken language, builds connections in the brain during the early and preadolescent years pre-eminently so.
5. *Psychological:* Language and the development of thought are inseparable. Learning is a social process, and high-quality talk helps to scaffold the student's understanding from what is currently known to what has yet to be known.
6. *Pedagogical:* Research shows that cognitively enriching talk engages students' attention and motivation, increases time on task, and produces measurable learning gains.
7. *Political:* Democracies need citizens who can argue, reason, challenge, question, present cases, and evaluate those cases. Democracies decline when citizens listen rather talk, and when they comply rather than debate.

---

## Observations on a Talk-Centred Classroom: Michelle

"Nothing is more fun than sitting in a circle and playing with people who are really into it."

— Kathy Mattea

"Oral language as the centre of the literacy program has changed the way my students look at learning," Michelle confirms. "It has really created a transformation of how I teach and how students feel in the classroom. Each year, just like you, I have a classroom composed of students with varying needs. Talk as the centre of the learning environment has created a cultural shift. It has significantly increased student engagement. As my students emphatically say, 'Is this *work*? 'Cause it is fun!' Oral language activities *are* fun. They also help make student thinking visible. Because of this, my job as an assessor of learning is much more manageable and authentic.

"Dialogic teaching has had a great impact on my teaching practice, something that can be summed up in four words: **release of teacher control**. As a teacher, you do not need to know everything, and your way is not always the right way. You need to have the courage to let go and give students the freedom to express their own ideas on and perceptions of a story or a conversation topic. When students are focused on ideas or topics they have had a hand in choosing, it brings engagement and progress to a whole new level.

"When students display lack of motivation, this indicates a call for help, and it is my responsibility to find ways that will enable them to learn. If students engage in their own creative process through oral language–based activities, they can imagine the end product, and as a result they take the initiative and begin the steps to get there.

"Allan Luke (2012) says that we as teachers need to develop 'a broad repertoire of instructional strategies and a kind of assessment of literacy so that we can actually see the kids, see the target competency, knowledge and skills and then put that repertoire in place.' An oral language–based classroom affects and changes the learning and demonstrates student potential that traditional workshop-style literacy classrooms do not showcase.

"In addition, Community Circle has become more than just an opening ritual. It changed my classroom physically, which, in turn, changed the whole atmosphere of the classroom. There is no longer a 'front of the class' from which I teach — there is no front in a circle. The circle turns, and everyone gets a turn. The circle creates equality — we are all in it together. Even when Terry and I performed a Readers theatre script in the circle, we each played in role as one of the students, and as part of the circle, the audience was on a par with the performers. This is the way it is all day in the classroom. I have noticed that formerly reluctant speakers are talkers now, willing to take risks, willing to have their voices heard. Like the finches in Henry Finch's flock, they have an identity and are ready to make their mark.

"Creating a talk community — a vibrant classroom — has transformed the way my students see themselves: they are learners in a collaborative environment where all voices are heard and appreciated. They are equal partners. Students work together collaboratively and creatively to push each other's thinking, making them the instruments in the process. The whole purpose of the LOL classroom is to make students collaborators in charge of their own learning. I know that we can never underestimate our students . . . Creating an LOL classroom has enabled me to be the kind of teacher I wanted to be."

## Talking Like Walking: Student Voices

As Michelle has said, "Oral language as the centre of the literacy program has changed the way my students look at learning." Several of her students, most in Grade 3 and two in Grade 4 (Sadi and Jay) have articulated Michelle's observation clearly and *out loud*. The final four comments appeared earlier (Chapter 2) but are worth restating here. For these students and for the rest of Michelle's class, being part of a vibrant talk classroom has allowed them to express themselves in ways that break free of some of the box-like structures sometimes encountered in school. In particular, Jay's comment, that *talking is like walking*, illustrates his insight into how talk is dynamic: it can lead you to new places and new ways of seeing and thinking.

SADI: Talking makes a different kind of experience in class. Learning is fun and it seems easier too.
CHRIS: Talking helps us learn because we can explain our thinking and it is way easier than explaining on paper. When I talk, I can use bigger words and not worry about spelling.
DANA: Talk helps me learn because my teacher can understand my thinking. I love having conversations with my teacher.
PATRICK: It helps me think. I like listening to what my friends think. Sometimes we give each other ideas for our work. We can talk about what

we are learning. My work is better when I can talk about it instead of just writing stuff down.

LUCY: Talk is like music. Your mouth is an instrument.

ALI: YES! You're expressing the song of your emotions.

CALI: Listening is like a circle, 'cause you're always listening. It never really stops.

Finally, we are brought full circle:

JAY: Talking is like walking. You can move around, walk around, and you don't always know where you might end up.

We opened this book with Alexis Deacon's story of Henry Finch, a red finch Viviane Schwarz depicted in the form of an individual thumbprint. In the story, Henry Finch begins to really think for himself. He then moves on from the sameness of his flock, and *through the power of communication*, he conquers the beast that threatened them all. He discovers his own individuality and, ultimately, his own greatness!

That is what Literacy experienced Out Loud does for our students.

# Acknowledgments

Grateful acknowledgment is made to the following for permission to quote previously published material:

Terry Campbell and Michelle Hlusek: *Storytelling and Story Writing: Using a Different Kind of Pencil* (Research Monograph No. 20, 2009).

Candlewick Press: Excerpt from I AM HENRY FINCH. Text copyright © 2015 by Alexis Deacon. Illustrations copyright © 2015 by Viviane Schwarz. Reproduced by permission of the publisher, Candlewick Press, Somerville, MA, on behalf of Walker Books, London.

Loris Lesynski, *Dirty Dog Boogie*. Text and illustrations copyright ©1999 by Loris Lesynski. Willowdale, ON: Annick Press.

Shelley Stagg Peterson: Excerpt from *Supporting Students' Vocabulary Development Through Play* (Research Monograph No. 62, 2016).

Pembroke Publishers, Markham, ON: Excerpts from *Balanced Literacy Essentials: Weaving Theory into Practice in Reading, Writing, and Talk*. Text copyright © 2012 by Michelann Parr and Terry Campbell.

# References

Akiwenzie-Damm, K. (2017, May 20). The debate is over. It's time for action. *The Globe and Mail*, pp. A12–A13.

Alexander, R. (2017). *Towards dialogic teaching: Rethinking classroom talk* (5th ed.). York, UK: Dialogos.

Allen, J. (2002). *On the same page: Shared reading beyond the primary grades*. Portland, ME: Stenhouse.

Almasi, J. F., Palmer, B. M., Garas, K., Cho, W. H., Shanahan, L., & Augustino, A. (2004). *A longitudinal investigation of the influence of peer discussion of text on reading development in grades K–3* [Final report submitted to the Institute of Education Sciences]. Washington, DC: U.S. Department of Education.

Alvermann, D. E., O'Brien, D. G., & Dillon, D. R. (1990). What teachers do when they say they're having a discussion following content reading assignments. *Reading Research Quarterly, 26,* 232–242.

Beck, I., McKeown, M. G., & Kucan, L. (2002). *Bringing words to life: Robust vocabulary instruction*. New York, NY: Guilford Press.

Beers, K. (2003). *When kids can't read, what teachers can do: A guide for teachers, 6 to 12*. Portsmouth, NH: Heinemann.

Bennett, B., & Rolheiser, C. (2001). *Beyond Monet*. Toronto, ON: Bookation.

Biemiller, A., & Boote, C. (2006). An effective method for building meaning vocabulary in primary grades. *Journal of Educational Psychology, 98*(1), 44–62.

Booth, D., & Barton, B. (2000). *Story works*. Markham, ON: Pembroke.

Boyd, M., & Galda, L. (2011). *Real talk in elementary classrooms: Effective oral language practice*. New York, NY: Guilford Press.

Britton, J. (1993). *Language and learning* (2nd ed.). Portsmouth, NH: Boynton/Cook.

Buchweitz, A. (2016). Language and reading development in the brain today: Neuromarkers and the case for prediction. *Journal of Pediatrics, 92*(3 Supplement 1), S8–S13.

Buscaglia, L. (1982). *Love*. Thorofare, NJ: Slack.

Calkins, L. (2001). *The art of teaching reading*. New York, NY: Longman.

Cambourne, B. (1988). *The whole story: Natural learning and the acquisition of literacy in the classroom*. Richmond Hill, ON: Scholastic.

Cambourne, B. (2000/2001). Conditions for literacy learning. *The Reading Teacher, 54*(4), 414–417.

Cambourne, B. (2017). Reclaiming or reframing? Getting the right conceptual metaphor for thinking about early literacy learning. In R. Meyer & K. Whitmore (Eds.), *Reclaiming early childhood literacies: Narratives of hope, power, and vision* (pp. 17–33). New York, NY: Routledge.

Campbell, T., Brownlee, A., & Renton, C. A. (2016). *Pedagogical documentation: Opening windows onto learning* (Research Monograph No. 61). What Works: Research into Practice. Retrieved from http://www.edu.gov.on.ca/eng/literacynumeracy/inspire/research/ww_pedagogicdoc.pdf

Campbell, T., & Hlusek, M. (2009). *Storytelling and story writing: Using a different kind of pencil* (Research Monograph No. 20). What Works? Research into Practice. Retrieved from www.edu.gov.on.ca/eng/literacynumeracy/inspire/research/ww_storytelling.pdf

Campbell, T., & Hlusek, M. (2015). Storytelling for fluency and flair: A performance based approach. *The Reading Teacher, 69*(2), 157–161.

Cazden, C. (1988/2001). *Classroom discourse: The language of teaching and learning.* Portsmouth, NH: Heinemann.

Clay, M. (2004). Talking, reading, and writing. *Journal of Reading Recovery, 3*(2), 1–15.

Copple, C., & Bredekamp, S. (2009). *Developmentally appropriate practice in early childhood programs serving children from birth through age 8.* Washington, DC: National Association for the Education of Young Children.

Cremin, T., & Maybin, J. (2013). Children's and teachers' creativity in and through language. In K. Hall, T. Cremin, B. Comber, & L. C. Moll (Eds.), *International handbook of research on children's literacy, learning and culture* (pp. 275–290). Chichester, UK: Wiley-Blackwell.

Dickinson, D. K. Griffith, J. A., Golinkoff, R. M., & Hirsh-Pasek, K. (2012). How reading books fosters language development around the world. *Child Development Research, 2012,* 1–15. doi:10.1155/2012/602807

Edwards, T., & Westgate, P. G. (1994). *Investigating classroom talk.* London, UK: Falmer Press.

Egan, K. (1993). Narrative and learning: A voyage of implications. *Linguistics and Education, 5*(2), 119–126.

Eisner, E. W. (2002). *The arts and the creation of mind.* New Haven, CT: Yale University Press.

Ferguson, K. (2014). *Performing poetry: Using drama to increase the comprehension of poetry* (Research Monograph No. 52). What Works? Research into Practice. Retrieved from http://www.edu.gov.on.ca/eng/literacynumeracy/inspire/research/WW_PerformPoetry.pdf

Garrett, T., & O'Connor, D. (2010). Readers theater: "Hold on, let's read it again." *Teaching Exceptional Children, 43*(1), 6–13.

Graves, M. F., & Watts-Taffe, S. (2008). For the love of words: Fostering word consciousness in young readers. *The Reading Teacher, 62*(3), 185–193.

Greenfader, C. M., & Brouillette, L. (2013). Boosting language skills of English learners through dramatization and movement. *The Reading Teacher, 67*(3), 171–180.

Harste, J. C., & Burke, C. L. (1988). *Creating classrooms for authors.* Portsmouth, NH: Heinemann.

Heath, S. B. (2004). Learning language and strategic thinking through the arts. *Reading Research Quarterly, 39*(3), 338–342.

Heath, S. B. (2013). The hand of play in literacy learning. In K. Hall, T. Cremin, B. Comber, & Moll, L (Eds.), *International handbook of research on children's literacy, learning and culture* (pp. 184–198). Chichester, UK: Wiley-Blackwell.

Heathcote, D., & Bolton, G. (1994). *Drama for learning: Dorothy Heathcote's Mantle of the Expert approach to education.* Portsmouth, NH: Heinemann.

Hoffman, J. L. (2011). Coconstructing meaning: Interactive literary discussions in kindergarten read-alouds. *The Reading Teacher, (65)*3, 183–194.

Hudson, A. K. (2016). Get them talking! Using student-led book talks in the primary grades. *The Reading Teacher, 70*(2), 221–225.

Jackson, J. T., Jenkins, K., & January-Vance, K. (2014). *Using readers theatre to promote fluency in struggling readers.* Paper presented at World Literacy Summit 2014, Oxford, UK.

Kalantzis, M., & Cope, B. (2012). *Literacies.* Cambridge, NY: Cambridge University Press.

Keeshig, L. (1990, January 26). Stop stealing native stories. *The Globe and Mail.* Retrieved from tgam.ca/stopstealing

LaBrocca, R., & Morrow, L. M. (2016). Embedding vocabulary instruction into the art experience. *The Reading Teacher, 70*(2), 149–158. doi:10.1002/trtr.1488

Luke, A. (2012). *Leaders in educational thought: Allan Luke on innovative assessment.* Retrieved from Curriculum.org

Maloch, B. (2002). Scaffolding student talk: One teacher's role in literature discussion groups. *Reading Research Quarterly, 37,* 94–112.

McIntyre, E. (2007). Story discussion in the primary grades: Balancing authenticity and explicit teaching. *The Reading Teacher, 60*(7), 610–620.

Myhill, D., Jones, S., & Hopper, R. (2006). *Talking, listening, learning: Effective talk in the primary classroom.* Berkshire, UK: Open University Press.

O'Connor, J. S. (2004). *Wordplaygrounds: Reading, writing, and performing poetry in the English classroom.* Urbana, IL: National Council of Teachers of English.

Ontario Ministry of Education. (2003). *A guide to effective instruction in reading, Kindergarten to Grade 3.* Toronto, ON: Author.

Ontario Ministry of Education. (2006). *The Ontario curriculum, grades 1–8: Language.* Retrieved from http://www.edu.gov.on.ca/eng/curriculum/elementary/language18currb.pdf

Ontario Ministry of Education. (2008). *A guide to effective literacy instruction, grades 4 to 6.* Toronto, ON: Author.

Ontario Ministry of Education. (2010). *Growing success.* Retrieved from http://www.edu.gov.on.ca/eng/policyfunding/growSuccess.pdf

Ontario Ministry of Education. (2010–2011). The full day early learning kindergarten program (*draft version*). Retrieved from http://edu.gov.on.ca/eng/curriculum/elementary/kindergarten_english_june3.pdf

Ontario Ministry of Education. (2016a). *Growing success — The Kindergarten addendum: Assessment, evaluation, and reporting in Ontario schools.* Retrieved from www.edu.gov.on.ca/eng/policyfunding/success.html

Ontario Ministry of Education. (2016b). *The Kindergarten program.* Retrieved from http://www.edu.gov.on.ca/eng/curriculum/elementary/kindergarten.html

Paley, V. (1997). *The girl with the brown crayon: How children use stories to shape their lives.* Cambridge, MA: Harvard University Press.

Parr, M., & Campbell, T. (2012). *Balanced literacy essentials: Weaving theory into practice for successful instruction in reading, writing, and talk.* Markham, ON: Pembroke.

Pascal, C. (2009). *Every child, every opportunity: Curriculum and pedagogy for the early learning program* (A compendium report to *With our best future in mind: Implementing early learning in Ontario*). Toronto, ON: Queen's Printer for Ontario.

Peterson, R., & Eeds, M. (1990/2007). *Grand conversations: Literature groups in action.* New York, NY: Scholastic.

Peterson, S. S. (2016). *Supporting students' vocabulary development through play* (Research Monograph No. 62). What Works: Research into Practice. Retrieved from http://www.edu.gov.on.ca/eng/literacynumeracy/inspire/research/ww_vocabulary.pdf

Peterson, S. S., & Swartz, L. (2008). *Good books matter.* Markham, ON: Pembroke.

Piaget, J. (1962). *Play, dreams, and imitation in childhood.* New York, NY: W.W. Norton.

Rasinski, T. (2006). Reading fluency instruction: Moving beyond accuracy, automaticity, and prosody. *The Reading Teacher, 59*(7), 704–706.

Routman, R. (2003). *Reading essentials: The specifics you need to teach reading well.* Portsmouth, ME: Heinemann.

Rubin, D. L. (1990). Introduction: Ways of talking about talking and learning. In S. Hynds & D. L. Rubin (Eds.), *Perspectives on talk and learning* (pp. 1–17). Urbana, IL: National Council of Teachers of English.

Rutledge, P. B. (2011, January). The psychological power of storytelling. *Psychology Today*. Retrieved from https://www.psychologytoday.com/blog/positively-media/201101/the-psychological-power-storytelling

Sawyer, R. (1942/1970). *The way of the storyteller*. New York, NY: Penguin Books.

Shanker, S. (2013). *Calm, alert, and learning*. Don Mills, ON: Pearson.

Shaywitz, S. (2003). *Overcoming dyslexia: A new and complete science based program for reading problems at any level*. New York, NY: Knopf.

Smagorinsky, P. (2001). If meaning is constructed, what is it made of? Toward a cultural theory of reading. *Review of Educational Research, 71*(1), 133–169.

Stahl, S. (2005). Four problems with teaching word meanings (and what to do to make vocabulary an integral part of instruction). In E. H. Hiebert & M. L. Kamil (Eds.), *Teaching and learning vocabulary: Bringing research to practice* (pp. 95–114). Mahwah, NJ: Lawrence Erlbaum.

Swartz, L. (2014). *Dramathemes* (4th ed). Markham, ON: Pembroke.

Vygotsky, L. S. (1971). *Thought and language*. Cambridge, MA: MIT Press.

Vygotsky, L. S. (1978). *Mind in society*. Cambridge, MA: Harvard University Press.

Vygotsky, L. S. (1987). Thinking and speech (N. Minick, Trans.). In R. Rieber & A. Carton (Eds.), *Collected works* [of L. S. Vygotsky] (Vol. 1, pp. 53–91). New York, NY: Plenum.

Wells, G. (1999). *Dialogic inquiry: Toward a sociocultural practice and theory of education*. Cambridge, UK: Cambridge University Press.

Wells, G. (2009). *The meaning makers: Learning to talk and talking to learn* (2nd ed.). Toronto, ON: Multilingual Matters.

Willis, J. (2006). *Research-based strategies to ignite student learning: Insights from a neurologist and classroom teacher*. Alexandria, VA: ASCD.

Worthy, J. (2005). *Readers theater for building fluency: Strategies and scripts for making the most of this highly effective, motivating, and research-based approach to oral reading*. Toronto, ON: Scholastic.

Worthy, J., & Prater, K. (2002). "I thought about it all night": Readers theatre for reading fluency and motivation. *The Reading Teacher, 56*(3), 294–297.

Young, C., & Rasinski, T. (2009). Implementing readers theatre as an approach to classroom reading fluency instruction. *The Reading Teacher, 63*(1), 4–13.

Zak, P. J. (2014, October). Why your brain loves good storytelling. *Harvard Business Review*. Retrieved from https://hbr.org/2014/10/why-your-brain-loves-good-storytelling.

# Index

*Abel's Island*, 83–84
accountable talk, 23
action words, 54
*Alexander and the Wind-up Mouse*, 21–22
*Anansi and the Moss-Covered Rock*, 97–98
anchor charts, 27
*And Tango Makes Three*, 65
anecdotal storytelling, 93–95
Applause, Applause, 56
*Asha's Mums*, 65
assessment
    choral speaking and dramatization, 79, 87
    oral communication, 28–29
    pedagogical communication, 27–28
    talk, 27–29
    teachers, talk and, 21
attentive listening, 28
audience awareness, 104–5
audience feedback, 107
Authors Share (Author's Chair), 44–45
"Away to the River," 85

blogging, 63
book talks, 44
brain imaging, 7
*Buttercup's Lovely Day*, 49–50

Carousel (strategy), 42
character traits, 54
choral speaking and dramatization
    anchor chart, 78
    assessment, 79
    described, 77
    poetry, 79
    small-group, 78
    "The Three Billy Goats Gruff" example, 77–79
    whole-class, 77–78
*The Chronicles of Harris Burdick*, 69

circle stories, 92–93
community building
    caring, 17–18
    families and, 17
    oral language and, 9–18
    story sharing and, 16–17
Community Circle
    connections, 12
    described, 7
    developing questions for, 13
    going around, 13
    good talk and, 24, 25
    moral teachings, 12
    setting the tone, 11–14
    symbolic objects at centre, 12
    talking stick, 11, 15–16
    value of, 14
control, 20, 116
conversation, 6
creativity
    described, 47–48
    playing with language, 57–58
    poetry, 48–52
    texts and words, 53–55
    tips, 57–58
    vocabulary, 55–57
*The Crow's Tale*, 33–38, 55, 90
cultural appreciation, 90
cultural appropriation, 89–90
culture
    Community Circle and, 14
    respect for, 90
    story selection and, 89–90

debates, 23–24
descriptive feedback, 28
discussion equity, 7–8
dopamine, 7–8

*The Dot*, 25–26
drama
    choral speaking, 77–79
    described, 75–76
    dimensions, 77
    everyday activities, 80–81
    improvisation, 82
    interviewing in role, 83–84
    introducing activities, 85
    mentor texts, 84
    minimal scripts, 81–82
    nursery rhymes, 82–83
    oral communication and, 76–77
    play centres, 80–81
    poetry, 79
    question-and-answer dialogues, 84
    strategies, 77
    tableaux, 85
    warm-ups and focusing strategies, 80
drawing and talking, 45

evaluative questions, 40
evocative texts
    described, 61
    read-alouds and, 68–71

*Fables* (Lobel), 98
favorite place stories, 93
fingerprint art, 10
focusing fingerplay, 80
"Fog," 49
*Four Feet, Two Sandals*, 61, 66–67, 72
*Frederick*, 11, 61

games, 56–57
"Goldilocks and the Three Bears," 61
good talk
    Community Circle and, 24, 25
    described, 23
    guidelines, 27
    inspiring and supporting student talk, 25–27
    need for model, 23
    strategies for cultivating, 23–27
grand conversation, 10, 44

*Hana's Suitcase*, 25
homonyms, 54–55
*Hooray for Diffendoofer Day!*, 56
*How to Catch a Star*, 32, 66, 71

*I Am Henry Finch*, 9–11, 72
*I Am Not a Number*, 67, 72
*I Want My Hat Back*, 61, 66, 72, 106–7
Idea Completion, 57
idioms, 57

*Images of Nature: Canadian Poets and the Group of Seven*, 70
*Imagine a Day*, 49–52, 61, 70, 71
*Imagine a Night*, 49–51, 61, 70
improvisation drama, 82
inferential questions, 40
informal debates, 23–24
inquiry learning, 84
Inside-Outside Circle, 41
interactive discussion, 60
interviewing in role, 83–84
IRE sequence, 21

*Journey*, 38–39, 71, 72

learning story, 28
*The Legend of the Lady Slipper*, 38
listening, 23, 28, 30, 78, 91, 104–5
literacy
    brain imaging and, 7
    classroom talk and, 8
    common elements, 60
    defined, 6
    *it* factor, 6
    oral language and, 6, 29
    pillars of, 93
    talk and, 6

*Marianthe's Story: Painted Words, Spoken Memories*, 16–17
*Max's Words*, 53
mentor texts, 84
mime strategies, 80
minimal scripts, 81–82
*Miss Alaineus: A Vocabulary Disaster*, 54–55, 57
*The Most Magnificent Thing*, 54, 64, 65, 71
multimodal poetry, 48–53
multimodal storytelling, 97–98
multimodal texts, 6
*My Two Blankets*, 53–54
*The Mysteries of Harris Burdick*, 61, 69

*The Name of the Tree*, 38
name stories, 93
noise, 20
*Nokum Is My Teacher*, 81
non-verbal cues, 77
nursery rhymes, 82–83
*The Nutmeg Princess*, 71

object stories, 93
*Ooko*, 84, 96
oral family heritage, 16
oral language/communication
    assessment, 28–29
    brain imaging and, 7
    community building and, 16–17

compass, 8
conversation and, 6
creating community with, 9–18
drama and, 76–77
importance of, 5, 6
learning through, 8
literacy and, 6, 29
play and, 57–58
storytelling and, 91

partner talk strategies
    effective use of, 40
    Inside-Outside Circle, 41
    Say Something, 41
pedagogical documentation, 27–28
picture books, 73–74
Place Mat (strategy), 42–43
play contexts (activity centres), 55
poetry
    choral speaking and dramatization, 79
    creativity and, 48
    multimodal poetry, 48–53
problem-based texts
    described, 61
    read-alouds and, 66–68
provocative and controversial texts
    after read-aloud, 63–64
    before read-aloud, 62
    described, 60–61
    during read-aloud, 63
    exploring controversies around, 64–66
    follow-up texts, 64
    reasons for using, 61
    talking about ideas, 62–64
punch, pause and paint strategy, 78
puns, 57

question-and-answer dialogues, 84

read-alouds
    activities after, 53, 54
    after strategies, 72
    before strategies, 71
    book selections, 73–74
    during strategies, 71–72
    evocative texts, 61, 68–70
    fictional texts, 16–17
    optimizing impact of, 59–61
    problem-based texts, 61, 66–68
    provocative and controversial texts, 60–61, 62–66
    selecting books, 60
    sparking talk about words, 53–55
    students' views on, 72–73
Readers theatre
    audience feedback, 107

co-creating scripts, 110–11
    demonstrating, 106–8
    described, 104–5
    getting started, 105–6
    independent circles, 111
    Kindergarten and, 106
    listening and audience awareness, 104–5
    reading fluency and, 104
    resources, 112
    small groups, 107–8
    steps for success, 108–9
    student-adapted scripts, 110
    student-composed scripts, 111
    success criteria, 110
    talk circles and, 103
    "The Talkative Tortoise," 113–14
real discussions, 20, 21–23, 44
real talk, 20
recitation, 21, 60
*The Red Lemon*, 61, 66
rereading, 92, 104
respectful talk, 26–27
retelling, 91
role-plays
    good talk and, 24
    interviewing in role, 83–84
*The Rough-Face Girl*, 38

Say Something, 41
*Scaredy Squirrel*, 42
scripts
    student-adapted, 110
    student-composed, 111
self-portrait storytelling, 95–97
sense (of story), 58, 91
sentence frames, 23–24
Seven Sacred Grandfather teachings, 12
*17 Things I'm Not Allowed to Do Anymore*, 62–65, 71
shadow puppets, 97–98
Sketch to Stretch *Plus*
    *The Crow's Tale* example, 33–38
    described, 31–33
    read-alouds and, 72
small-group discussion strategies
    Carousel, 42
    Place Mat, 42–43
    success criteria for self-assessment, 43
*Smoky Night*, 33
*So, What's It Like to Be a Cat?*, 83
Socratic circle, 12
speaking and listening anchor chart, 78
*The Stamp Collector*, 66
story sharing/storytelling
    anecdotal storytelling, 93–95
    assessment checklist, 102

benefits of, 91–92
connecting to families and communities, 17
cultural considerations, 89–90
getting started, 92–93
methods, 93–101
oral family heritage, 16
participation activities, 92–93
performance, 98–100
read-aloud fictional text models, 16–17
rereading, 92
respect, 90
retelling, 91
self-portrait storytelling, 95–97
shadow puppets and, 97–98
steps, 99
tales for telling/retelling, 100–101
Storytellers of Canada, 15
student-led book talks, 44
synthesis questions, 40

tableaux, 85
talk
    accountable talk, 23
    assessing, 27–29
    challenges of managing, 11
    drawing and, 45
    good talk, 23–27
    literacy and, 6
    positive emotional connections through, 7–8
    real talk, 20
    respectful talk, 26–27
    students' views on, 30
    teachers' involvement in, 29
    teachers' mistrust of, 19–21
talk (dialogic) classroom
    assessment, 21
    beauty of, 115–17
    conditions for supporting, 29–30
    control, 20, 116
    good talk, 23–27
    noise, 20
    observations, 116–17
    real discussions, 21–23
    reasons for, 116
    student voices, 117–18
    teacher talk, 21–22
    teachers' mistrust of talk, 19–21
talk strategies
    partner strategies, 40–41
    Sketch to Stretch Plus, 31–38
    small-group discussion strategies, 41–43
    talking and drawing, 45
    whole-group discussions and sharing, 44–45
    wordless books, 38–40

"The Talkative Tortoise" (Readers theatre), 113–14
talking stick, 11, 15–16
task cards, 25–26
teacher talk, 21–22
"The Three Billy Goats Gruff," 77–79, 86
The Three Questions, 37
The Top Secret Files of Mother Goose, 83
touchstone text, 10
town hall discussion, 72
Tuesday, 39–40, 61, 71

vocabulary
    augmenting with words, 55–58
    games, 56–57
    play contexts, 55
    puns and idioms, 57
    repeated exposure to words, 56
    students illustrating new words, 56
    teaching explicitly, 55–56
vocal effects, 77
voice warm-ups, 80

walking the wall, 56
The Watertower, 65–66
What Do You Do with an Idea?, 64
whole-group discussions
    Authors Share (Author's Chair), 44–45
    choral speaking, 77–78
    grand conversations, 44
    student-led book talks, 44
    wordless books, 38–39
Why the Banana Split, 57
Woolvs in the Sitee, 66
Word Associations, 57
word wall, 56
wordless books
    described, 38
    read-alouds, 74
    small-group discussion, 39–40
    students producing, 40
    talk strategy, 38–40
    whole-group discussion, 38–39
words
    action words and character traits, 54
    collecting and categorizing, 53
    gaining gift of, 53–54
    games with, 56–57
    homonyms and, 54–55
    illustrating new words, 56
    repeated exposure to, 56
    sense, 58
    using texts to spark talk about, 53–55
    vocabulary and, 55–58